VESSELS

Vessels

A Love Story

DANIEL RAEBURN

W. W. NORTON & COMPANY
Independent Publishers Since 1923
New York London

Printed in the United States of America
First Edition

Portions of this book previously appeared in slightly
different form in *The New Yorker.*

For information about permission to reproduce selections from this book,
write to Permissions, W. W. Norton & Company, Inc., 500 Fifth Avenue,
New York, NY 10110

For information about special discounts for bulk purchases, please contact
W. W. Norton Special Sales at
specialsales@wwnorton.com or 800-233-4830

Manufacturing by Berryville Graphics
Book design by Helene Berinsky
Production manager: Julia Druskin

Library of Congress Cataloging-in-Publication Data

Names: Raeburn, Daniel K., author.
Title: Vessels : a love story / Daniel Raeburn.
Description: First edition. | New York :
W.W. Norton & Company, Inc.,
[2016]
Identifiers: LCCN 2015032512 | ISBN 9780393285383 (hardcover)
Subjects: LCSH: Raeburn, Daniel K.,—Health. | Raeburn, Bekah. |
Miscarriage‹Patients-‹United States‹Biography. |
Pregnant women‹United
States‹Biography. | Husband and wife.
Classification: LCC RG648 .R34 2016 |
DDC 618.3/92092—dc23 LC record
available at http://lccn.loc.gov/2015032512

W. W. Norton & Company, Inc.
500 Fifth Avenue, New York, N.Y. 10110
www.wwnorton.com

W. W. Norton & Company Ltd.
Castle House, 75/76 Wells Street, London W1T 3QT

1 2 3 4 5 6 7 8 9 10

For Bekah

The vessel that he made of clay was
marred in the hand of the potter.

—Jeremiah 18:4

One

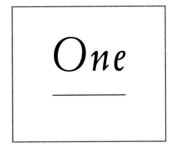

I MET BEKAH ON MEMORIAL DAY. A PARTY. SHE WAS SHORT, with umber hair and freckles. Endless freckles. A guy holding a plate of ribs said something to her and she smiled a little, lopsidedly. She had her doubts, but she was enjoying nursing them.

Our hosts saw the change come over my face. He made documentaries; his wife was a therapist. I'd met them eight years ago, through a newspaper ad. The documentarian had wanted a roommate; instead he got a friend. He became my way in to Chicago: the Get Me High, the Crash Palace, the Lounge Ax. The Empty Bottle, where I stood in the corner and talked about the books I ought to write. He rocked from side to side while he listened, like one of the boxers he made movies about. My flurries amused him, probably because he was older than me. He indulged me in a way people my own age didn't. So did the therapist. At their wedding they drank from a clay jar that they passed to their families, then their family of friends. Then they smashed the jar. Klezmorim warbled. As we hoisted the two in their chairs, I thought about my parents. They'd made my childhood; had these two helped me make an adulthood?

They wanted to make something out of me and this woman at their Memorial Day party. They knew it wasn't good for me to be alone.

I can't believe I never thought of you two before, the therapist said.

The therapist had one eyelid that drooped; it made her look like she'd been struck by something, but remained unfazed. She led me across the back porch.

Rebekah: This is Dan. Dan, Rebekah. I can't believe you two haven't met before.

Neither could I. Years later a friend asked, How'd you know Bekah was the one?

I didn't know how; I just knew. I told my friend, Of all the women I've ever met, she's the first one who felt like family.

I'd see why the night Bekah and I were sitting on the edge of our bed, looking at a photo album. A boy of four or five looked back: freckles, pug nose, umber bowl cut. He could've been Bekah's twin, but she didn't have a twin. I did. A fraternal one. One I wasn't that close to, even though he and I had been closer to each other than we were to anyone.

I'd never understood what had come between us. The last time I'd seen him he'd said that the two of us should step outside and settle this with our fists. Once and for all.

Settle what, I'd said.

Everything!

Bekah saw the rhyme too.

Your brother, she said. He and I looked so much alike.

We turned the page.

FAMILY. I'd had a few, depending on how you counted. The first one ended in Iowa, when I was ten. My mom left my dad for a preacher who'd lost his faith. The only explanation my twin and I got for this came from our dad, who said, Your mom and I don't love each other anymore.

He sounded like he couldn't believe it, and knew that that was why he had to.

The next family ended six years later, in Texas. My mom came to breakfast with a violet ring around her eye.

It's not what you think, she said. I was so upset last night that I walked into a lamp.

The preacher stared into his bowl. I looked down at mine. My twin had already moved back to Iowa, leaving me feeling like I couldn't. I couldn't abandon my mom. Not in Texas.

I have to move back to Dad's, I said. I've been thinking about it for a long time.

The preacher stood.

You don't have to leave, he said. I will.

He'd left us a dozen times before, but this time he didn't come back. My mom and I went into town to see a landlady, who saw the ring behind my mom's sunglasses.

You and your boy move on in. We'll worry about that deposit after you get settled.

We used my savings account to pay for our moving van.

I DIDN'T want to run the risk of anything like that again. So I didn't. I never wanted to get married, just like I never wanted to have kids. But I always, always wanted the thing that made kids. I made it with kids my age, kids of the largest generation of kids in history. Baby boomers' kids. First a girl whose dad was a photograph in a shoebox, her mom the someone who'd given her away. Then a girl whose dad beat her mom to death. Her mom was still alive, though, and still married to her dad: After the medics brought her back to life, she remarried the man who'd killed her. Then a girl whose mom had used her as collateral in a drug deal. One whose mom had set her up to be raped by an uncle. One whose dad kept slaves. Three of them. They'd volunteered for the job. They wore padlocks on the chains around their necks.

As kids, these girlfriends had tried their hardest to act like adults; now that they were, they were still trying. So was I. When I was thirteen the joints in our house weren't mine; they were my mom's. The porn mags were the preacher's. I didn't sneak out of the house at night, but he did. I had no desire to relive that childhood.

Is that why I was still trying to have it? I was thirty-two years old when I met Bekah, and I still went everywhere on my bicycle. I collected comic books. I put out a fanzine about them called *The Imp.* That's what people who didn't know me called me: the Imp. Cute. I took pride in it, sometimes. Weekends weren't easy. I'd roam the city on my bike and hitch it outside a bar. Later I'd get back in the saddle and pedal back to my apartment and my bathroom mirror, where I'd notice that one side of my face hung lower than the other. I'd started smoking again.

Bekah worked freelance, doing photography props and wardrobe. Nights she poured drinks at a pub, not only for customers. She thought she might be turning into someone like her dad, who also drank. Not that the two of them were close. She hadn't spoken to him since she found out that he'd been visiting Chicago without telling her, to date a woman who was even younger than she was.

One night she was walking back to her place, her tips in her pocket, when a man holding a knife stepped onto the sidewalk in front of her.

Your money or your life.

She hesitated, which says something about her finances.

It's ten years in jail to me, he said. But it's your life.

She hesitated, which says something about that life. Put it this way: If she'd been pushing a baby stroller, she'd have handed him the money. She turned and ran. He didn't chase her; that's why she was alive on Memorial Day.

I didn't tell her that instead of writing books, I'd ended up writing about other people's. That I was a thwarted artist. I'd tell her later; talking about it now might guarantee that there wouldn't be a later. I said I was a writer. She was a potter. *Potter* sounded good. When my twin had done it he'd called it ceramics or ceramic art. He'd made pieces; Bekah threw pots. Everything was a pot, even if it was a plate. She only made pots people could use, and she tried to make them embody something she called The Unknown Craftsman. It was an invention, she said, but true anyway: this idea that a craft should be free of the signs of craft. When you remove the markers of your personality, you reveal the pot's true character, and your own.

A pot should be its own signature, she said. That's why I stopped signing mine.

She'd also stopped making them, but she didn't tell me that. Not yet. That would've meant telling me that she'd won a couple awards. That she'd been sent to an island where potters gathered, where she'd built a pot from coils, rolled ropes of clay that she wound around each other in whorls until they made what looked like a giant thumbprint. This pot sold at auction for more than any other craft on the island.

If Bekah had told me this, she'd have bragged. She doesn't do that. Worse, she'd have had to explain what came next: sales, commissions, recognition, and the realization that she'd lost whatever had made her want to throw pots in the first place.

How do you explain that a part of you isn't part of you anymore? You talk about anything but. As we talked I focused on her hands. They were small and spotted, with fingernails that had been rounded like pebbles. Clay had made them older than the rest of her.

Where had I seen them before?

I'd remember where when my dad's mom died. At Grandma's funeral I talked about her hands, which had been small and spotted and always occupied. When they were empty they seemed preoccupied. Fidgety, to use a word Grandma had used. The thing about her hands was how plain they'd been. Then I said that I'd met someone.

I'd fallen in love, but it didn't feel like falling. I'd been falling; now I'd stopped. Someone had caught me, someone who had hands like Grandma's.

After the funeral my twin met this woman who'd once looked more like him than I had. When I took her hand in mine, he nearly did too.

You're right, he said. Her hands.

Bekah didn't say anything. We'd compared her body to a dead one.

At the Memorial Day party a look came over her. She excused herself. Half a beer later the documentarian and the therapist stepped in.

She's leaving.

I rushed onto the back porch.

Hey! Do you want to go out sometime? On a date?

She looked back. So did the guy next to her. Her date.

I work at the Inner Town, she said casually. You could stop by.

I rode my bike eleven miles there and back. Twice. Both times she wasn't working. The bartender wouldn't give me a last name or next shift. No stalkers.

You could stop by: I let the neutrality of her words win. Soon I couldn't remember her face, only what she'd looked like. My impression of her. The more I dwelled on the impression, the more it looked like I'd never see her again.

The summer passed. September 11th dawned. I was writing about Mexican comic books when the phone rang. My nearest friend, a painter who lived next door. His apartment's floor plan was the mirror image of mine.

Mate? Can you come over here and sit with me?

Watching people jump from the Twin Towers, I couldn't speak. Words would admit reality. The painter said enough for both of us. He wept, too. He admitted the grief I shared, but couldn't share. That day he became not only my nearest friend, but my closest friend. My mate.

Six weeks later my phone rang.

Remember me? a woman's voice said. Do you want to go out sometime? On a date?

On the 11th she'd forced herself to step away from the television and stand outside. The sky: There wasn't a thing in it. One of her thoughts was of me. She was still waiting for me to stop by. Why wait? She'd be thirty-two years old in a few weeks. She'd do something she'd never done before: make the first move. She got my phone number from the documentarian, then took a month and a half working up the nerve to dial.

She said, This phone call is my birthday present to myself.

I'd just marked my own birthday by not marking it at all. Here was what I'd wanted: the woman I couldn't really remember, but couldn't forget. I felt chosen.

She lived on Iowa Avenue, on a block that wasn't patrolled by police, but by kids. Teenagers. They wore white T-shirts that hung to their knees and baseball caps with their brims off-kilter. One leaned on a cane. Another rocked in his wheelchair.

Bekah opened her door and I smelled soap, wet tea leaves, the bowlful of plums on her table. Her eyes were blue and gray, like the Great Lake I'd ridden next to to get there.

You shaved your beard.

I don't remember another word we said. I remember what we talked about: our lives. They were ours now, even if they weren't of our own making. Now that they'd led to this they seemed like they were about more than just themselves; now they were about life itself. We'd found a witness. We must've known even then that loving this witness would be hard, and a job the witness himself had already failed at. All the more reason to do it. We ended the night with a kiss. After she'd closed her door on me I had the feeling I was by myself, but not alone.

That was Wednesday. Saturday she showed me her pots, which she'd stacked inside each other in columns that clinked and swayed as she carried them to her kitchen table. Each pot was as plain as a stone. Unique, but also a reminder of the one before it, and the one after it. Potters call this the hand. It's like handwriting: easy to recognize and almost impossible to fake, or describe. Bekah's pots were bulbous, like they'd been breathed into. Like they held something, even though they were empty.

There are three tests for a pot, she said. First, when you throw it, it has to feel right in your hand. Then, after you fire it, it has to come out looking like something you'd want to keep. Then comes the third test: You have to live with it. You have to use it. This is the real test.

One cup had a handle shaped like half a valentine. I lifted it and felt the stone it had been turned into.

That one's probably my favorite, she said.

She'd bisque fired it in a gas kiln that turned the gray clay pink; then she buried it with dozens of other pots in an outdoor kiln. She fed wood into a fire at one end of the kiln until the temperature got up to 2400 degrees Fahrenheit; hotter than lava. When the fire died and the kiln cooled, the cup was the color of a fallen oak leaf. That's because it was oak. The minerals in the wood had turned into ash, and the ash had fused to the clay, giving it a brown skin, along with what you might call birthmarks: spots, moles, scars. Ash had given the clay life, or something that looked like it.

Look inside, she said.

A skeleton.

A baby snake, she said. Between the time I loaded the kiln and when I fired it, the snake slithered in, coiled up, and went to sleep.

The fossilized spine was a broken question mark.

On our next date she gave me my Christmas present. A bowl. We sat at my kitchen table while she told me how she'd made it. She said that a potter has to throw the same pot over and over until its shape becomes second nature, until she forms it so fluently that even her slipups seem like they were done on purpose. I turned the pot in my hands as she pointed out the accidents that had happened. On the wheel its lip had relaxed from a strict circle to a lazier roundness. In the kiln the iron glaze on the pot next to it had vaporized, ghosting a blush across one side. That's what Bekah cherished. Mistakes made the clay human.

A drawing of a cracked egg was taped to the wall above her bed. I fell asleep under it. In the morning she dropped me off downtown, where I caught a bus back to Iowa City. I was washing the Christmas dishes when I said, So, Dad. I think I've met the one.

He stopped drying the iron skillet.

Really.

He sounded unable to believe me, and for that reason unable not to.

Did I believe me? A few months later Bekah said something about us moving in together. I don't remember what I said next, but I know I didn't say it. I blurted it.

It's not that I didn't want to live with her; I didn't want to live with anyone. Except for her, of course. But not yet. Not so fast. We couldn't rush this. We had too much to lose.

At a certain point you should just know, she said. And if you don't know, then you have to ask yourself why you don't.

I did know; I just wanted to be sure.

She said, If we're not living together by the end of this year, it'll be over.

I was riding down Iowa Avenue one night when I saw the kids on her corner surround a car. A woman and a girl of about twelve were inside it, wearing seat belts. A boy rapped on the girl's window with the barrel of his pistol. A few days later someone smashed out the rear window of Bekah's car. Her next-door neighbor said, We been wondering who did that.

She smiled. She was our age, but she was a grandma.

Bekah and I loaded everything she had into a moving van. As we pulled away a kid slapped a high-five full of bills into that grandma's palm. From under the bills he fingered a small foil packet and slipped it into his pocket.

It turns out that Bekah's hair wasn't umber, but dyed umber. It had turned gray when she was sixteen. No one knew why. Heredity. She cooked potfuls of food but she didn't eat much. Her appetite had died. Even in summer she shivered under our goose down comforter. Urinary tract infections made her double over. One drove her to the nearest emergency room. When I got there a nurse was injecting her with something.

I could see Bekah's eyesight recede. The doctor strode in and put his hands on her pelvis.

Tell me where is pain.

I can't feel anything. Not now. Not anymore.

Maybe cramp? That time month?

The bill was already six months' rent. She didn't have health insurance. The doctor shrugged at a nurse and said, *Ya nyeh zna-yoo.*

I didn't need to understand Russian to know what he meant. We checked out.

Her eyebrows started to vanish. What spooked me were her hands. They'd gotten numb. When I traced my fingertips along her forearm, instead of feeling her skin quicken, I felt nothing. No, not nothing: something unfeeling. One night her hand fell on me and I woke up, my skin crawling. I thought I'd been touched by something dead.

Falling asleep, she called it. It was because she'd spent

so many years wedging clay. Loading racks of pots in and out of the kiln. She turned each hand with the other, trying to knead them back to life. She got them to work, but as soon as she went back to sleep, they did too.

This isn't me, she said. I'm not like this. I'm not myself.

I WAS. Being me meant knowing that Bekah was the one, but being unable to believe in what I knew. One morning we were at our kitchen table, talking about where our relationship was going, or not going. Not where Bekah wanted it to: somewhere. Anywhere. We were on the brink of arguing about our last argument on the subject when it hit me: I'd had this conversation with every one of my girlfriends, and I didn't want to have it again. Not ever. I interrupted.

Let's get married.

Our eyes met. I couldn't believe I'd said it either. I couldn't marry someone because she wore overalls. Because she pulled her hair back with a rubber band, baring the skin behind her ears. Because I had a sense that she was part of my childhood, even though she'd been missing from it. These weren't reasons. This wasn't a matter of reason. Did I even need a reason for wanting to spend the rest of my life with this woman?

Bekah's pupils were like two moons eclipsing blue suns. Like she'd seen a light and been blinded by it at the same time.

Okay.

The word sounded tiny. We went into the bedroom and undressed each other. I laid her pale body across the bed. Then I remembered: her diaphragm. It was still in its clamshell under the bathroom sink. The moment felt too holy for that. Too sacred. I plunged in.

That was our engagement. A month later was her birthday. We drove to a town on the banks of the Mississippi, where we checked into an old-fashioned rooming house next to the railroad tracks.

What about protection, I said.

Don't worry. It's not that time. I can tell.

The bedsprings screeched. We stopped to listen for the hush of another guest listening, but we didn't hear anything, which made the fear worse. A freight train drew near. As it got louder we started up again, faster and faster until boxcars roared past the window, sucking in the curtains, making the washbasin and water pitcher on the bedside table buzz against each other. After the train was gone we lay there, panting.

Our wedding, we said. We should have it here.

That was her birthday. Twenty-one days later was mine.

When it was over she sat me down in our living room; I thought she was about to give me another present.

I'm pregnant.

She wanted to keep it. I wanted to be angry. I knew that she hadn't been able to tell if it was that time of her cycle or not.

Thanks for ruining my life, I said.

She spent the night with her back to me. I spent it thinking about that life. It was the one I'd had since I was born; the only one I'd known. The end of it seemed like the end of everything. Like suicide. It was tempting. In the morning I told Bekah I'd drop out of the creative writing program I'd applied to. I'd give up freelancing. Find a steady job with health insurance. I had to. I wanted to.

No, she said. I will. I'll figure it out.

We didn't argue. We finished breakfast and drove down to Arkansas, where one of Bekah's sisters met us at her door, eight months pregnant. Her husband held up a beer; Bekah declined. Casually.

You're pregnant, her sister said.

We took a walk through leathery, rustling leaves. Hearing Bekah's sister and her husband talk about their future, I realized that birth wasn't the end of life; it was its beginning. A revelation so obvious I didn't dare say it out loud.

The baby was due nine months after Bekah's birthday,

on the Fourth of July. On the drive back to Chicago we crossed the Mississippi.

Huckleberry, I said. If he's a boy.

She smiled a little, lopsidedly. She didn't like the idea, but she liked that I'd had it.

Maybe just Huck, she said.

We couldn't afford health care, but the state provided it so long as Bekah's income stayed where it was. Now we really couldn't afford to get married. At our first ultrasound Bekah's second heart drummed relentlessly; our hearts raced along with it. Two weeks before Christmas it stopped. The doctors couldn't say why. Miscarriages are usually for the best: That's what everyone said. We said it too.

But I meant it.

The fetus didn't come out, so a doctor scraped it out. Afterward an orderly delivered Bekah to me in a wheelchair. Bekah's hair seemed grayer, her face paler. Her hands held onto the plastic bag that had her belongings. This was a scene from the end of our life together, not its beginning. Was I remembering things before they'd actually happened?

She stayed in bed for two days. Then she packed her bags and drove back to the Mississippi, where she took a freelance job in Saint Louis. For ten days she zipped women into white wedding gowns. She arranged flowers in their hands and turned them to face the camera. She wrote me to say that I'd been many things, but that I'd been there. This had made her feel trapped, but now she felt something more.

Expanded, she said. Not with pregnancy, but with something else.

WHAT was that something? Christmas Eve was the documentarian's birthday. He and the therapist had had a boy, and I held their son, felt his weight. Felt the responsibility that wouldn't be mine anymore. Bekah had wanted it; I'd only wanted to want it.

I spent the night on our matchmakers' couch. In the morning I walked the six miles back to our apartment, beside the Lake as flat as a nickel. Our child had had no life. We had nothing to mourn.

Is that why I was crying?

Two

SPRING WAS STILL WINTER. THE BARE TREES ALONG THE Lake stood out like branches of lightning. Bekah was walking her sister's dog when two boys on the sidelines of a basketball court sprinted toward her. One had a baseball bat.

She knew that if she ran, she'd be giving them what they wanted. Not money. Power, a power the powerless can easily imagine. They wanted to terrorize her. The one with the bat raised it; he was rearing back when she forced herself to take a step toward him. She made herself smile.

Hi.

The boys slid to a stop. The one with the bat spun around, dismayed. His friends back at the court jeered. The other boy lowered his eyes.

What kinda dog is that.

The hound stood at the end of her leash, wagging her tail.

Beagle.

The boys walked away. The beagle tugged Bekah on. Ten minutes later they were back at our apartment. Bekah didn't call the cops. The boys hadn't committed a crime.

Why not? Not because she was pregnant. They didn't know that; neither did she. Not yet. Not for another week. But she'd been thinking about being pregnant, thinking about it a lot. The thought of it was already real. Is that why she didn't run the way she had from the man with the knife?

To me, the baby wasn't real. Not yet. After Bekah told me that she was pregnant I called it It, and thought of it the way I'd thought of Huck: as an idea, one as unlikely to survive as him, or every other idea that came into my head. Then Bekah had her twenty-week ultrasound. It was a she. She looked like a white dwarf in a distant galaxy. We were halfway to zero.

Her name came to me as I fell asleep, her hands and feet drumming against Bekah's belly and my palm. Good night, Irene: I'll see you in my dreams. I didn't remember anything about the song other than the chorus. *Irene Raeburn*: Bekah also liked the sound of it. The name stuck. I don't know if I saw her in my dreams or not. My dreams were like the warm air beneath our blankets: gone the second I got out of bed.

One morning Bekah woke up in pain, blood between

her legs. At the emergency room the resident had to shout over the howling man handcuffed to the bed next to ours. Placenta abruptia, she said. She couldn't say why. Too many possibilities. We asked her what were Irene's chances of surviving until January, when she was due. The resident couldn't say. Maybe fifty-fifty. She sent Bekah to a nutritionist, who held up a carton of milk and a box of cereal.

This is what you should buy at the store.

Bekah left thinking the words you're not supposed to say around kids. In a suburb twenty miles north of us she found a midwife who worked with a doctor. Normally their hospital didn't accept people who didn't have insurance, but because Bekah was pregnant, the state paid for it. Again. Our new doctor listened to Bekah. She sent her to an endocrinologist. The endocrinologist tapped Bekah's knee with a little silver hammer. The knee reacted slowly.

You have an autoimmune disorder.

She ordered a test of Bekah's thyroid gland. When the results came back she noticed that the lab had run the test twice; the first time, the numbers were so low they'd thought they might've made a mistake. But there was no mistake. The endocrinologist prescribed Bekah white pills. After Bekah took them the numbness in her hands started to go away. Sensation came back, followed by feeling. For the first time in years, Bekah felt like herself.

I DON'T know what scared me more: that we'd lose our baby, or that we'd have it. That fall, when we passed around a scuffed plastic infant at our birthing class, I sensed something without feeling it, like someone behind me had been about to touch me.

Old friends wrote to say that this Rebekah they'd heard about could only be good for me. Same with this baby. The Dan they'd known would soon be gone forever. They were happy for me.

One letter came from the girl whose dad had been a photograph in a shoebox, her mom the someone who'd given her away. My first. She'd worn black clothes, black hair, black sunglasses. She'd been different, and we'd been different together. After school we lay on the mattress on the floor of her room, listening to a cassette tape of a man who wore a dress sing about pilgrimage and passion. That's what we did. That and smoke. I knew that smoking killed; that's why I did it. I wanted to die with her.

We also did what we called It. The last time was at the house of a boy named Chance. My rubber broke. We drove a hundred miles to Dallas, where a woman in an unmarked office gave us a morning-after pill. A few weeks later my first climbed onto the back of a motorcycle straddled by a guy who wore a Mohawk and a kilt and wound her arms around his waist. I went back to my room and got the shoebox that held every letter she'd ever written me and carried it to the dumpster, where I abandoned it. If anyone had asked me what I was crying about, I'd have said, Over someone I never knew.

Another letter was from the girl whose mom had used her as collateral in a drug deal. She was a high school teacher, and she'd left me for one of her students. Killing my feelings for her had felt like smothering a crying baby. Like I wasn't only the smotherer, but also the baby.

Now I was grateful for these dead ends. Without them I'd never have met Bekah. The story of my life had finally led me to a point.

On the eve of Christmas Eve we went to her aunt's annual party. Around midnight Bekah had to sit down. She felt dizzy. Queasy. But she took a startled pleasure in caressing her thrumming belly.

Irene's kicking like crazy. She's never kicked this hard. Never.

Any day now, I said, any day.

I shrugged into my coat, offered her my hand.

Christmas Eve was the documentarian's birthday. Another party. Bekah's face was as white as the moon that followed us along Lake Shore Drive. She said, I think I'm coming down with something.

A man at the party said that she looked heavenly; he took her belly into his hands with his fingertips, as though it were a balloon. When he raised his glass to our matchmakers, Bekah and I did too.

Mazel tov!

On the way back to our place Bekah said, I'm definitely coming down with something.

Then she slept.

Christmas morning I woke up before dawn. Snow floated like down from a burst pillow. I drove to my dad's house, Bekah asleep in the passenger seat, Irene inside her. For the first time I wasn't going home for Christmas. Home wasn't where I'd grown up; my family wasn't the ones that had made me. It was the one I'd made, the one in the car. I sped through frozen fields lined with broken corn. At the edge of one a pipe stuck up from the earth, spewing flames. The heat made the falling snow float up, like ash. A green sign said *Peace Road.*

I remember Peace Road because I don't remember anything after it. I don't remember crossing the Mississippi or being met at the door by my dad and stepmom. The coffee, bacon, and orange juice. The fire hissing in their fireplace, the crackling of unwrapping presents. The staticky telephone call to my mom, then my twin. The new wool sweater scratchy around my neck and wrists as I digested the prologue to a book. I know these things happened, but only because they happen every year. After Peace Road, the day's a zero.

We woke up the next day in my old bedroom. Bekah said, The baby didn't kick yesterday.

Silence.

Did she move at all? I said. Just a little?

It's hard to tell. I think so. Maybe.

She put her hands on her mound and lay still.

You've come down with something, I said. So's the baby. You've been sleeping a lot; so's she. She's sleeping. We've already got a doctor's appointment first thing tomorrow morning.

She nodded. Not agreeing, consenting. Her face was blank. We got dressed and went downstairs. My dad and stepmom, spoons clinking against crockery, comments I forgot as soon as they were made. Bekah and I finished our tea and set out on a walk. The sky was white. Leaves scuttled past. We let gravity lead us downhill to the university, where I'd read the books that had made me see that life wasn't about my life. Where the end of my childhood had been conceived.

I'd lived here for twelve years, in ten different places. I wanted to show them to Bekah, starting with that red brick one over there, on the side of that hill. As I pointed I realized that I couldn't remember the name of the street the place was on. I'd also forgotten the names of the streets that led to it. I was a stranger now in the town I knew by heart.

I've been here before, Bekah said.

A muddy river snaked beside us, cold as chocolate milk. Up the riverbank was a heap of sawed logs, white, fragrant fingerprints at their ends. Past the woodpile was a limestone hut half sunk into the ground. Steps led down to a door that had been bricked shut. The arch around the bricks was blackened.

Two guys in coveralls were watching over the hut. One had a staff. Bekah walked up to them and said Hi. They nodded.

She said, Fifteen years ago my pottery teacher in college brought us here to see this kiln.

Kill, said the one with the staff.

Just as millers work in a mill, not a miln, some potters say kill, not kiln. These two had made it a shibboleth. When Bekah asked them about their firing they were polite, but that's all. They didn't offer their names. At the end of a silent spell the one with the staff thunked it against the ground, as though he were trying to wake someone up.

We walked away. Years later Bekah told me that as we'd

walked, she'd felt her womb contract. But because she'd never had contractions before, she didn't recognize them, only the need to keep walking to ease them. She walked with her hands in her pockets. In my pockets; she was wearing my goose down vest. It went halfway to her knees, but she was so pregnant that it was the only thing that fit her. She'd never been bigger, and never looked smaller. More precious. I was about to tell her this when she looked up at me.

I want to go home.

That's all we said. We walked back to my dad's house and gathered our presents. As we stood in their doorway, taking our leave, Bekah took a step toward my dad and stepmom. She made herself smile.

Next time we see you we'll have a baby.

Darkness fell as we crossed the Mississippi. A passing car honked. Then another. A driver pointed at the rear of our car. I pulled over. Our taillights had burned out. The next gas station didn't sell taillight bulbs, and the service station was closed for the holiday. So I drove on, trying not to imagine what it would be like to be driving behind us and see us too late. I didn't turn on our emergency flashers. The streetlamps would provide enough light. This wasn't an emergency.

I don't remember sliding into bed that night, or what we did or didn't say when Bekah left first thing in the morning for her doctor's appointment. I don't remember the phone ringing. I remember raising it to my ear.

A silence. Bekah's. Irene was dead. I knew it. When Bekah said my name, the crack in her voice confirmed it.

A quiet African man drove me in his taxi, his radio issuing news of the tsunami that had just struck the other side of the world. Thousands dead. So many the authorities would never be able to count them all. The South Side slipped by. Concrete sky, the frozen Lake. Stone and steel downtown. People photographing themselves shopping, ice-skating. Standing under trees whose bare stalks branched like capillaries for brains that had gone missing.

Our midwife's receptionist showed me to where Bekah was waiting. Bekah's pants were unzipped. She'd been running from room to room, from test to test, carrying her parka and holding up her pants. She took me into her arms and held me. Fiercely, as though I were her child.

Our midwife asked Bekah to consider childbirth. Birth would mean a day or two or three of labor, but it would give her better odds of giving birth next time.

Next time. I couldn't imagine a time after this.

Our midwife said, Women who've had to go through this, and chose to go through with birth, are grateful that they did. Later.

Okay.

Bekah's voice sounded tiny.

We checked into the maternity ward. I thought that we didn't belong with the normal parents, but the head resident said that stillbirth was birth and that we were parents.

But what you're going through sucks, she said. It just sucks.

The room came with a candy-colored baby blanket and a beanie. I told the nurse who injected Bekah with hormones that we wouldn't need the clothes.

They're for the photos, she said.

I stared at her. She knew that our baby was dead.

We won't be needing photos.

She took the clothes away. After dark she brought them back. She set them on a table in the corner and petted them, as though putting them down for the night. She whispered:

In case you change your mind.

In the middle of the night voices murmured through the wall, growing louder, rushed. A baby cried. Cheers, clapping. Bekah rustled, then shifted. She was a shadow. So was I.

In the morning a social worker sat in front of us. She had to make sure that we were certain about the photos.

I know this sounds weird, she said, but parents in your

situation who decline the photographs often return, begging us to please let them see a photo of their child. Don't you at least want the option to see photos—not now, but someday?

No, I said.

Bekah shook her head. We signed papers promising not to sue anyone.

The social worker left her card, along with a pamphlet she called literature. The literature had a drawing of a teddy bear dressed in overalls. A butterfly had landed on the teddy bear's nose, forcing him to cross his eyes and smile. Inside were black-and-white photos of a woman propped up in a hospital bed, holding an inert baby. None of the photos showed the baby's face. Beneath them were poems written by bereaved parents. Bekah dropped the literature onto the nightstand, but I read every artless word. One boldfaced quotation struck me:

"The main thing in life is not to be afraid to be human."

Beneath the quote, a name I'd never heard.

In the afternoon one of Bekah's sisters walked in, along with Bekah's best friend, and saw me sitting next to Bekah, wearing a new sweater and reading aloud to her. Just like we were having a baby. They burst into tears. Then they sat with us as we drank tea from paper cups. Our midwife put on a cardigan and joined us. Night was falling, but nobody turned on a light. A spell was falling; none of us wanted to dispel it.

We told our own birth stories. I stood up to tell mine. My mom and dad didn't know that my mom was carrying twins; neither did the doctor who delivered us. When he broke the news to my dad, the doctor, who was Japanese, said, So sorry. You have not one but two healthy boys.

He bowed.

I only charge you for one.

I bowed. The women laughed.

The labor got heavy. All Bekah could do was breathe. She sat still, half in this world, half in the next one, the one that would deliver her baby. Bekah's best friend cried; she said she ought to be going. So did Bekah's sister. They left. Then Bekah's sister came back, her eyes as big as eggs.

I want to stay.

She stayed as Bekah was possessed by what it takes to bear a child. Possessed. Bekah told me later that the only reason that she could bear the pain was because it made her forget that our baby would be born dead. Me too. I couldn't imagine what was happening, even though it *was* happening, right before my eyes. Whenever I did remember that our baby would be dead, I told myself that the birth would be the end of that death, not its beginning.

Blood sloshed out of Bekah and dripped onto the floor.

She's crowning.

Our midwife pressed warm towels between Bekah's legs to try to stop the tearing. I took one of Bekah's legs and her sister took the other. Our midwife bent between, ready to catch.

Someone once said that William Carlos Williams was sitting by the bed of a patient when she died. He looked out the window and saw a red wheelbarrow glazed with rainwater beside white chickens. I saw a salt-stained sidewalk under the funnel of a streetlamp. A beige plastic armrest beside a blue blanket. My black boot slipping in red blood.

Irene was in the breech; she came out rump first.

Push.

Bekah pushed. She pushed again. She pushed so hard that the red hole in the center of Irene's exposed butt opened. A black turd slithered out.

Bekah expelled her and I glimpsed the corpse flop into the hands of our midwife. The nurse snipped the bobbing umbilical cord and whisked the body out of sight.

I bent down and said, That was the bravest thing I have ever seen.

Bekah tried to make a noise. To nod. She closed her eyes. I turned to face our baby.

She looked like a photograph of a dead baby. Like the ones in the newspaper, ones of the wars overseas. Greasy black hair covered her arms and legs. Her nose looked like it had been driven back into her skull; it was a raw, upturned pug.

The nurse had set the body under a heat lamp so that it would stay warm to the touch. She asked me if I wanted to cut the remaining tendril of umbilical cord. I did. It felt like cutting through someone's finger.

She nudged Irene's pudenda. A beautiful girl, she said. With perfect little girl parts.

She traced a finger over Irene's nose.

That's because she was breech, she said. Coming out backward, babies always get their noses bent out of shape.

Irene had mooned us and shat at us. Gotten her nose bent out of shape. She even smelled like a sourpuss: sulfurous, vinegary. She was a pickled imp, delivered from whatever she'd died fighting. I gathered my girl into my arms.

The nurse who'd induced Bekah had tried to warn me. The tone, she'd said: After they've been dead for a few days, they don't have the tone. The tone is missing.

Irene's face splayed flat in my hand, like an overripe tomato. I put my thumbs above her eyelids and eased them up, thinking I'd look into her eyes. But the milky slivers awed me. I stopped. The plates of her skull grated as I cupped my palm and rounded her face to its likeness, which I recognized. It wasn't like looking into a mirror. In a mirror you see your reflection; in your child you finally see how everyone else has seen you.

Bekah opened her eyes. I handed her our girl. She looked down.

Take her! Can you take her!

Bekah's sister scooped up Irene and walked her around the room, rocking her. Singing to her. I ran my hands up and down Bekah's back, dampening her quaking.

Where was the afterbirth? It was supposed to slide out at the end of the umbilical cord like a lung. Either it was stuck to the uterus, or the uterus was refusing to let go of it. The umbilical cord dangled between Bekah's legs. Our midwife tugged on it and it snapped.

That's not supposed to happen, she said. I mean it happens, but it's rare.

She called in our doctor. Our doctor inserted one hand into Bekah. She braced herself and pulled. Pulled harder. Bekah's sister and I tried to restrain Bekah. I felt something tear. Our doctor slid back, holding a piece of organ. She handed it to the nurse and reinserted her hand.

I don't want you to have to leave this room and check into surgery, she said. Not now, not after all that you've been through.

Bekah went so stiff she absorbed my trembling. This time I didn't look at anything, not until I felt our doctor step back. She stripped the slick glove from her hand.

I think that's it.

She asked our midwife and the nurse to gather up the afterbirth and send it to the lab. While they did that, Bekah started shivering. Shaking. Her sister and I buried her under a mound of blankets. The nurse stuck more needles into her and Bekah slipped into sleep, her eyelashes a pair of parentheses that had toppled, releasing whatever secret they'd held.

Bekah's sister left. She didn't come back. It was late now and I was alone with my family. Bekah's face floated above the blankets that swaddled her. Across the room, Irene lay alone in the glow of the heat lamp.

The night nurse stepped in. They were coming to take my baby away. Did I want to spend just a little more time with her?

No, I said. We've had our goodbyes.

I WOKE up in the middle of the night. A voice had sung the song with a twist: Good night, Irene; I'll see you, but only in my dreams.

Only in my dreams. Never in real life.

I remembered hearing the song on a jukebox. Over film credits. At a party in college. A friend who had chronic throat problems had set up a piano in the party's backyard and croaked it out as his last song for the night. As he sang I'd stood there with my beer, wondering, Where have I heard this song before?

Fifteen years in the future, that's where. I fell back asleep. In my dream Bekah was sobbing. When I woke up she was sobbing. I went back to dreaming. At first light I woke up and felt a second of equanimity. Tranquillity. Then I remembered: Our daughter was dead. Bekah was alive. It was harder to believe that Bekah was alive.

Months later I told Bekah that I was sorry for going back to sleep that night, of all nights. She looked at me like she didn't recognize me anymore.

I wasn't crying because of Irene. I was crying for you.

THE hospital served us breakfast. Milk and eggs. We stepped into the shower, where I washed her. Gingerly, the way a newlywed would. We put on the clothes we'd worn before the birthday and drove back to our place, slowly, as though we had a baby in the empty safety seat and a newborn awareness that an accident could strike any moment. Bekah limped up the three flights of stairs to our door.

There was a box in front of it, addressed in the hand of a friend.

Like me, this friend was a twin. Unlike me, she wasn't. Her twin had been born dead. As a girl she'd been spooked by the way her mom stared at her, like her mom wasn't seeing her, but her dead twin instead.

Bekah and I knew what was inside the box she'd sent. I opened it anyway. Bekah considered each jumper, each bib, each onesie, before folding it and tucking it into Irene's dresser, next to Irene's cradle and Irene's toys. We got into bed and spooned together. Bekah's breasts wept milk, so she bound them.

If we'd lived two hundred years ago, when Illinois was still prairie, Bekah would've had a dozen or more kids. The ones who survived would've lived to thirty-five or so. Our age. The age Bekah probably would've died, probably while giving birth. But at least she'd have been allowed to bury Irene with her own two hands. She could've worn a black veil or torn her clothes so people would know not to walk into the elevator and tell her, Smile; things can't be that bad. Or stop her on the sidewalk and say, You must've had your baby by now.

Nobody would've told her that stillbirth was a tragedy.

Back then every woman had babies who died. They still do. Half of all fertilized eggs die, usually before the woman knows she's pregnant. All she knows is that her period is late and more clotted than usual. A heavy period.

I let go of Bekah and went into the kitchen. Scrambled eggs spat in the hot skillet. I cut the rubbery thing in two and brought her her half.

She lay on her side with her arms around herself. The look on her face wasn't new. She looked like she'd always suspected that life would come to this, and couldn't help believing that by suspecting it, she'd created it. She bled so heavily that I had to put one of Irene's cloth diapers under her. When she finally fell asleep I left the room and closed the door gently.

The buzzer buzzed. Flowers. The first arrangement was from Bekah's grandpa, Poppa. Poppa had been an obstetrician; he'd delivered dead babies. He knew their silence. That's why he'd sent flowers; they were the admission that there's nothing to say.

The buzzer buzzed. Another arrangement, this one from our friend the biology teacher, and her husband the cartoonist. The cartoonist's birthday had been Irene's. When I called to thank them he told me about his great-great-grandmother, who'd settled on the prairie, just like Laura Ingalls Wilder, who'd also borne a dead baby, and whose books my mom had already given us to read to Irene. Reading his great-great-grandmother's diary, the cartoonist had been surprised by how common a certain sentence was.

Baby died, he said. Baby died. It was like a refrain.

One arrangement never arrived. My dad had had it delivered to the hospital, but we'd never gotten it, and he called me wondering why. He'd already asked the hospital and the florist. Someone had mistaken it for a bouquet of congratulations and intercepted it to spare us; that was my guess, but I didn't say that. My dad needed a mystery that could be solved.

There was one last arrangement. Our doctor and our midwife had had to go home, drop their keys on the counter, and answer the question, So how was work? That thought got Bekah to pick up the phone and dial a florist. She sent *them* flowers.

The buzzer buzzed. Bekah's aunts. They wrapped us in dramatic, almost frantic hugs and gave us sacks of food. One yanked open a bag of tortilla chips and the chips burst out, skittering across the floor. The aunts shrieked, not because of the chips, but because of what had happened to me and Bekah. Bekah knew this, but I didn't. I couldn't stop being who I was before the birthday. I'd written one essay arguing that an artist had been an asshole, and another arguing that an artist had been an asshole, but an asshole I admired. That's who I'd been. Now I was nothing but what I'd been. I followed Bekah's aunts and their presents into our living room.

The *living* room. What was that supposed to mean?

One aunt talked until the other picked up the sentence and ran with it. Finally one turned to me and said, Dan, you know how you were wondering what to write about next. Now you have something to write about.

I excused myself, went into my study, and shut the door. My daughter had stopped living; I'd stopped being her dad. I believed this.

After Bekah's aunts left Bekah's fever came back, so hot that she shook. I called our midwife.

No more visitors, she said. Strict bedrest.

The phone rang. People wanted to know. What, I wasn't sure. When I tried to talk about the birth it seemed more factual, but more unbelievable. Talking about it betrayed it. As long as I kept it to myself, I kept it alive. As soon as I tried to say it, it died.

The twinless twin who'd sent us the baby clothes cried the loudest. I told her not to worry. That we were doing okay. I consoled everyone who called to console us. It worked; I started to believe that I was okay.

The buzzer buzzed. Bekah's mom. She'd driven more than a thousand miles overnight to be with her firstborn.

For the next three weeks she did our shopping, cooking, and cleaning. She sewed new slipcovers for our furniture. She did almost everything, which made it clear that she couldn't really do anything to help. She cried.

Bekah thought that if anyone ought to be crying, it was her, not her mom. I have to start doing things for myself, she said. I'm not a baby!

She didn't want to work with anyone who'd known her before the birthday. When her fever receded she got dressed and rode a bus to the skyscrapers downtown, where she took a job in an office where no one knew anything about her but her name.

YEARS later I'd hear a lexicographer on the radio. I'd met her once, before Irene was born. A party. She'd held her baby against her hip. On the radio she was talking about me and Bekah: not us in particular, but people like us. There was a word for us. The problem was, the word didn't exist. If your spouse is dead you're a widow or a widower; if your parents are dead you're an orphan. But if your child is dead?

A lexical gap, she called it. Probably the most well-known. There was no prejudice behind it. Lots of people had tried to think up the word that could describe a parent who wasn't a parent. But none of these words had been adopted. None had survived.

THE results of the autopsy came. "Idiopathic stillbirth." I had to look up *idiopathic.* It's the same *idio-* that's in *idiot.* Own, personal, private. Idiosyncratic. She'd died for no apparent reason.

Bekah remembered being drunk before she found out that she was pregnant. She'd had high blood sugar and low blood sugar. Gestational diabetes. And those urinary tract infections. The antibiotics. Her hands. And that thyroid test: The results had been unbelievable.

I fixated on the song. It had come to me in the night, as unthinking as breathing, and I learned why. It's a traditional arrangement; no one knows who wrote it.

How could I have named her for no reason?

We tried to be strong, but if I cracked a joke, I laughed while our only child was dead. If she went out to see a friend, she abandoned me. By trying to be strong for each other we hurt each other, and by trying to be normal we grew numb. Talking about grief might add to it, so I kept quiet. So did she. We became closer to our baby, the thing we had in common, than to each other. Like all new parents.

After a month we got dressed for our first night out: dinner at the biology teacher's. She was seven and a half months pregnant. When we got near their driveway Bekah started to cry.

I can't do it. I can't.

I pulled over. Traffic whizzed by. For a month now we'd had her family living with us. Family! Yes, we'd needed them, yes, they'd been there for us. They'd made us, and we could never really be ourselves without them. But it was also true that we couldn't really be ourselves until we were apart from them. Free of them. We needed our friends too. Didn't she see that?

She did. She wanted to see our friends. But she didn't want them to see her.

She said, I just really hate myself right now.

I wanted to argue against this, but I didn't know how to without arguing. I dropped her at our door and drove back to our friends' house, where I picked at a casserole and talked about anything but.

The first friend to come to us after the birthday was the painter. He walked up to Bekah and tried to speak; instead he wept the way he'd wept on September 11th. Other people cried, but they cried for us. For our sake.

The painter cried for his sake. Because he'd never know Irene either. That was the only time that I didn't feel like I was alone.

Bekah remembers being surrounded. Cared for. Not me. Some friends never called or wrote again. Others acted ashamed, as though they had no right to breathe while our baby didn't. None of them knew what to say, especially the ones who couldn't stop talking. Eventually they'd run out of nothings to say; they'd realize that we couldn't think about anything but our newborn. Like all new parents.

On Valentine's Day we drove to my dad's house. After we took off our coats he took Bekah aside. I overheard his solemn murmur, her sniffle. I could almost feel their hug. That night I tried to talk to him. I couldn't. I blubbered, buried my face in my hands. I heard his chair scrape back from the table. Felt his hand on my shoulder.

Time for bed.

My dad's not unfeeling. When his big brother died he wept so hard I saw his shoulders shake from ten pews back. Not at the funeral, though. At the wedding three years later, when we were watching his dead brother's only daughter say, I do.

When we got back to Chicago I asked Bekah to go to a meeting of people like us. People who'd had miscarriages and stillbirths, babies they'd felt they had to abort or pull the plug on. We met in the hospital where Irene was born. Humming fluorescent lights, burnt coffee, a tray of untouched cookies. A ring of frightened faces with one angry one in the middle. A red one, right across the table from us. The woman looked like she'd actually suffered a blow.

When Bekah said our daughter's name a woman next to Bekah turned.

I'm Irene.

She looked like she was about to touch Bekah. She laid her palm against her own chest, stilling the impulse.

The woman across the table spoke up. You could tell that she'd been waiting, just waiting for her turn. She'd lost her girl, she said: Now everyone wanted her to pretend that her girl never existed. The rest of the room seconded her complaint. We finished each other's sentences. Society was on trial and we were the jury.

Everyone outside this room seemed to think that having another kid would somehow negate the loss of this one. That death was some kind of math problem you could solve with procreation. People were being supportive, but they were all secretly hoping that *it* would get better, that *things* would go back to normal, as if normal were an option, as if normal even existed anymore. If one more person told us to put it—it!—behind us, we might lose it.

I said, What do you say when people ask you if you have kids? If I say yes, they're going to ask about them. If I say no, I'm lying.

Nobody knew how to answer my question.

A woman spoke through her translator while her husband kneaded her hand. She'd been carrying twins. For five months everything was fine. Then one's heart stopped beating. He died, except he didn't die. His brother's heart came to his rescue, pumping enough blood for both of them. But that twin was going to die too; his heart couldn't take the strain. A specialist tried to extract the doomed brother so that his savior would live, but something went wrong. The translation wasn't clear, but in the operating room both boys wound up dead.

My heart, the dad said in English. It has been cut.

I cried, not because I felt for these parents, though I did. I cried with relief. Their stories were worse than mine. I was still lucky. We were still lucky. For the first time since the birthday I wasn't angry.

Bekah was. On the drive back to our apartment she said, That woman. She acted like she was the only one who'd ever lost someone.

I knew the one. Not the one with twins. The one who'd been waiting, just waiting for her turn. Who'd seemed to dare you to notice her, then damn you when you did.

I don't want to go back there, Bekah said. You can. I won't.

I never did. I must've known that a grief group wouldn't reconnect me to Irene. Grieving cut me off from her. That's why I did it. Grieving was my way of avoiding mourning.

I claimed Irene at a place that called itself a home. A man who called himself a mortician handed over paperwork, along with what he called cremains. A cardboard box. Inside the box, a tin; inside the tin, a baggie. A dog tag dangled from the baggie: MONTROSE CEMETERY 27683.

There wasn't a birth certificate; the law didn't allow it. No longer a fetus, not yet a newborn. Nothing.

I kept the baggie and threw out the box and the tin. I slipped the dog tag and the death certificate into an envelope and filed it under *Medical Bills*. After a minute I made a new file folder—*Irene Raeburn*—and filed it after *Investments*.

Her ashes weren't like the ashes in a fireplace. They were sandy, like the crumbled shells and bones that arc along the lakeshore. There wasn't much. About what you'd shake out of your shoes after a day at the beach.

We knew which pot would hold the ashes. A vase that could hold one flower. It had a small round foot, a fat middle, and an eye so small that you couldn't see into it. It looked like a top. Bekah had glazed it a glassy blue-gray, like ice under an overcast sky, then slashed a darker gray glaze around its shoulder. The darker glaze made crystals that looked like gray snowflakes. A few streaks of carbon were still stuck to the sides. The pot had also been through a furnace.

I sifted the ash through a sieve into a mixing bowl. I rolled a sheet of paper into a cone, inserted the narrow end into the eye of the pot, and poured in the ash. It hissed. I took the larger, unsifted bits from the sieve and dropped them into the eye one piece at a time. One lump was too large to fit through the eye; I put it aside. I'd make a second pile of the larger pieces, one I'd come back to later and—what? Smash with a hammer? But in the end there was only the one lump. I studied it. A molten zipper pull. I thought about keeping it until Bekah came back from work and reminded me that Irene had never been dressed in anything with a zipper. The zipper was from the body bag.

One night Bekah asked me for something in bed. Shyly, like it was an intimacy we'd never tried.

Tell me about her hands.

I remembered seeing Irene's hands, but I couldn't remember anything about them.

Describe them, she said. Her fingers. Were they all there?

I'd have noticed if they weren't. I said yes.

All ten?

Yes.

All small, she said. All perfect.

In the morning I drank my coffee and stared at the urn. I'd put it on its own little shelf in the kitchen, stoppered with a cork meant for a test tube. In my hands it had felt like a lodestone. Now that it was up on a shelf it had lost its pull. I fished in my desk drawer for the image taken at Irene's last ultrasound, five days before Christmas. The gathering of features was cloudy. She could've been anyone.

A few nights later Bekah said, She looked like a monster.

She had. That I couldn't forget.

Maybe Bekah thought of herself as the monster. The mother who'd rejected her child. Maybe. Maybe she did make a mistake when she asked us to please take her. But maybe that was a mistake she had to make. She'd been in labor for twenty-eight hours; if she wasn't near death, she was next to it. Literally. What if she'd stared it in the face?

Her job ate up her weekdays; weekends ate at something inside her. She stared out the window at scabs of snow. Plastic bags flapping in thorny trees. Blackbirds lighting and alighting on telephone wires like notes in a piece of idiotic music. She paid for studio time at our neighborhood art center. When she got back her hands were dull and gray, like stones. But they sparkled too. Silica glittered in their wrinkles. She seemed almost animated, almost like her old self.

The next weekend she came back in a grave mood. The instructor had told her, You can't mass produce stuff here.

She wasn't. Instead of trying to throw a perfect pot, she was trying to throw a hundred. One would turn out the way she wanted. This didn't waste clay; it improved it. After she pounded the pots down the clay would be ready to use again, like kneaded dough.

The instructor went back to paging through his magazine.

When Bekah fired the one she wanted, the glaze crawled off it.

She kept only a handful of pots. When I complimented them, I condescended to her. When I consoled her, I failed to argue against her disappointment. We argued anyway, even though my argument wasn't with her. I remembered her saying, This isn't me; I'm not myself. She wasn't. She sounded pessimistic, self-defeating. Like me. I couldn't accept my role in this, and I fought against it.

We fought in the kitchen, where our baby was and

wasn't. We began by listening dutifully to each other with our arms crossed, as though we were doing penance. Our voices rose until they mirrored each other, both insisting on the inverse of what the other insisted. After enough of this pointless reflection, Bekah raised the mug she'd been drinking from and flung it against the floor.

She didn't shatter our store-bought mugs. Only her own. I swept up the pieces and slid them clinking into the garbage. After another argument another night I took the cup with the snake inside it and stowed it in a drawer in my desk. That's why I'm drinking from it now.

One night Bekah said, You're not just angry. You're angry at me.

I'd managed to hide this, but only from myself.

I remembered our first big trip together. Zion, where we'd stepped inside a slit in the Earth's crust. The slit was a hundred feet deep, so narrow we'd had to walk single file. When our shoulders brushed against the stone, we were brushing against the Jurassic Era. We rounded a bend. A skeleton, ten feet above our heads. A fawn. A flash flood had lifted her up and driven her into a crease in the rock. We took a lot of photographs that day, but not of the fawn. We knew we'd never forget her.

We'd spent days in the canyons' mazes. Now she was sitting across the kitchen table from me. I learned one thing in the wilderness, I said: whenever I found myself lost, to stop and sit still until I could remember the last time I knew where I was and where I was going.

When was that for you, I said.

She was quiet.

For me, it was the morning I finished writing the *Imp* about Mexico. That, and the day I asked you to marry me.

Irene's birthday, she said. And the day after, when we got back from the hospital. Before we had to start seeing people.

She was right. All we'd had to do then was grieve. Now we had to live.

Or survive. At first I didn't recognize a guy who lived in our building. His head was shaved white, his scalp stitched together like the hide on a baseball. Kids, he said. Out front the other night. They didn't take his wallet. They'd just wanted to hit him.

A few days later somebody taped a notice to our lobby door. Kids had singled out more than thirty people at random and beaten them. Avoid leaving the building before school, after school, or during lunch hours. The warning faced in from our lobby window, so people who walked by couldn't read it. Whoever'd posted it didn't want the kids to know that they had people scared.

In April two girls jumped a woman. She was found next to her shattered cell phone, her baby crying in its stroller. Some of my neighbors were shocked: Girls had done this. I wasn't shocked. I'd seen girls tear each other's hair out. I'd stepped over clumps of bloody braids on the sidewalk. The next day seven kids beat a man. By the end of April more than forty people had been beaten. By the end of May, fifty-five.

Every weekday Bekah stood in front of the high school across the street, waiting for the bus that took her downtown. I didn't wait with her, and she didn't ask me to. That's how deadened we were. We'd eat breakfast and say, Bye. I'd hear the stairs groan, the lobby door bang shut. Then I'd listen to a piece of music that had been left for dead.

The man who wrote it was the youngest of eight kids, four of whom died. When he was nine his mom died. Then his dad died. He was sent to a conservatory, where he learned to compose and mourn at the same time. He grew up and had seven kids. Three died. His wife died. He remarried and had thirteen more kids. Seven died. Twenty kids, and ten died.

The music was an ecstasy of agony. It sounded like it

was agonizing over life itself. Was it really worth the living? I was asking myself this question, and no answer made sense. Sense wasn't the point. Sensations were. That's what the music gave me: the feeling that even though life itself means nothing, living is everything.

The cellist playing it had been born a hundred and twenty-eight years ago, on the day after Irene's birthday. When he came out his face was black, the umbilical cord a noose around his neck. He survived, but his mom's next baby didn't. It died. So did the next. And the next. And the next. And the next. And the next. And the next. And the next. Eight kids in a row died. At age twelve their brother found what I was listening to in a secondhand shop, where posterity had more or less left it. He took it back to his room and practiced it in private for twelve years. Then he played it in public. When he did, he resurrected it. We can't think about Bach's six suites for cello without thinking about the boy who adopted them: Pablo Casals.

I'd heard that name before. Where? I remembered the voice in my head, the one that's always been a part of me, but also apart from me, even though it's mine. An inkling led me across the room. I rolled open the drawer in my filing cabinet. There was the folder with Irene's name. Inside it was the booklet with the cross-eyed teddy bear. The literature. Inside that, the bald statement that had struck me:

"The main thing in life is not to be afraid to be human." Pablo Casals.

I listened to him and Bach religiously. I got rid of the records I'd grown up with. The historical record. Records by bands named for psychological disorders, insecticides, suicides. Bands whose names ended in *-ide*, period. Named after battlefields, combat, the 'Nam slang that meant zipped into a body bag. A record with a song about drinking black coffee and staring at the wall. The last time I'd listened to the song I'd been sixteen years old, driving my car sixty miles an hour upside down, in midair. Not on purpose, but not accidentally; it was an accident that was bound to happen. I was wearing an army field jacket and no seat belt. As the car and I turned end over end three times and crunched down onto the highway in front of oncoming traffic, black coffee and staring at the wall became the last words I'd ever hear.

But they weren't. An upside-down paramedic appeared.

You all right?

He couldn't believe it either.

In the twenty years since, I hadn't listened to the song. I didn't need to. I heard it in my head every time I drank black coffee and stared at the wall, which I've done every morning ever since.

I stacked my records in front of a record store clerk. He said, Would five hundred dollars be too much of an insult?

Yes, but I said No. Record stores had been my favorite form of financial suicide. One last time wouldn't kill me.

The only time I hesitated in this purge was when I came across my favorite album. A double album. Twin records, from the Twin Cities. I'd once told the documentarian that listening to them was like loading both barrels of a shotgun with black licorice, sticking them in your mouth, and pulling the trigger. The band had translated their name into the language of another country. It was Do You Remember?

The album had a junkyard on its cover. Crushed cars. I tossed it in with the rest. I'd always love it. That's why I had to get rid of it.

MOTHER's Day came and went. No one mentioned it. Bekah had her period. Before it had come every twenty-eight days; from now on, every thirty-two. She marked the starting date on our calendar. Two weeks later she stopped on her way out the door.

Today is baby-making day.

The stairs groaned; the lobby door banged shut. I went to the window and looked at the entrance to the high school. The girls' entrance. One shoved another and laughed. Another walked with her head down, lugging a horn.

In my hands that night Bekah's body felt softer, riper. I mounded mine over hers and pushed away a memory of the times I'd gazed at photos of mammary glands and birth canals, a tissue in one hand, like I was about to have a good cry. When I slid into the canal that Irene had come out of I remembered her birthday. Not the day itself; only my impression of it. Our bodies made a cradle; the rocking made me feel like we were making each other younger. Her eyes brightened. Her lips reddened. She flushed. Became someone she'd been before I met her, someone I'd only seen in photos and could never remember: a woman of twenty-seven, nineteen, seventeen. A girl who'd closed her eyes at night, hoping that the fantasy of one of her secret selves would come true. I put my mouth on her nipple and latched on. We reverted to our original, wordless state. Anyone awake next door heard us cry out. We fell apart, eggy and spent. Called each other baby. Slept like the dead.

On the Fourth of July we drove downstate to the town where Bekah was born, where we changed into black clothes and went to a place that called itself a home. There was the body of a woman I'd never even met. No one at her funeral was grieving. No one but me.

Three

THE NIGHT BEFORE OUR WEDDING, OUR MATCHMAKERS hosted a party in their backyard. I thought that one of our parents would stand up and offer a toast, but they didn't. They seemed separate, not only from each other, but from the crowd. The documentarian stood. He told everyone how on Memorial Day he and the therapist had slid me and Bekah together, hoping to join us. In honor of that day, they were serving beer and ribs. He stepped down and tapped me; it was my turn.

I raised my glass. When Bekah and I met, we were at the tail end of extended childhoods, hanging on to something that didn't exist anymore. Then we had Irene. By making us parents, she made us into a man and woman, and man and wife. She married us. Tomorrow was just a ceremony. It would confirm what had been born eight months ago.

I didn't say this, though. Our wedding wasn't about the

family we'd made. It was for the families who'd made us. So was this speech. For hopeful faces, and filling a pause I'd let go on for too long.

I said something for everyone, not Irene. I can't remember what.

We came together the next day in the courtyard of an art museum. I wore black, Bekah silver. I waited for her at the altar, next to her sisters and my twin. Our parents stood behind us, mine politely, Bekah's silently. After sixteen years her mom and dad still weren't speaking.

She walked down the aisle at sunset, escorted by her grandpa. Poppa had delivered babies for fifty years, and that night he delivered the one I couldn't help but think of as mine.

One of her bowls was on top of the altar. The wine in it looked like a black pupil in a green iris. Bekah lifted it to her lips and drank. So did I. I handed it to our families to circulate as a woman in a round collar stood in front of us, reciting vows we repeated in the silences that followed, our eyes swimming the way they'd swum the day I said, Let's get married. Together we repeated the final line:

Until death do us part.

I slid her finger into a ring; she slipped one onto mine. The painter brought her bowl back to the altar, empty. I thought about smashing it the way our matchmakers had, but I hadn't remembered to ask the woman in the round collar if I could do it, and to do it now might make it look like an accident, instead of a symbol of all accidents.

I'd left the one who'd wedded us out of our wedding.

I kissed the one I'd made her with: my wife. I danced with her, then her mom, then my mom. Then again with the mother of my child. Night fell. The courtyard became a space lit by a hundred candles. The band played gypsy jazz as kids raced around with lit sparklers, tracing silver spirals. The biology teacher, who was wearing her baby in a sling, like a pea in a pod, looked at me with the reflection of those sparks in her eyes and said, This night has made me feel sexier than I've felt in I don't know how long.

For our honeymoon Bekah and I hiked across New Hampshire. We were climbing Mount Lafayette when the long arm of a hurricane struck. The gale made the ground move as the tree roots beneath it flexed. I held onto the forest floor and watched a stone the size of an egg tremble in its mossy cradle, then pop out.

The storm passed. We crawled into our mummy bag.

When we got back to Chicago I started to write about Irene. When I looked up from the page I looked into my reflection in the glass that framed the inkblot over my desk.

My hands made a double fist in front of my mouth. I looked like I was praying for words, but also blocking a fountain of them.

Some of what I had to say wasn't mine. I'd found it by accident in Irene's room. The half room: That's what the real estate agent had called it. After I moved in I threw my empty boxes in it and called it the storage room. After Bekah moved in we called it the side room or the spare room. After she painted it white we called it the baby's room. After the baby we didn't call it anything. Bekah got rid of the baby's things, then her own.

Her pottery files filled the recycling bin. I picked up a file on top. It was an essay about a potter who wanted to be anonymous. That's because his pots weren't really his; other hands had dug the clay and wedged it, and gathered and chopped the wood that turned it into stone. Pots were shaped by a person, but they were the product of people. That's why shards in a dig mark the spot where a tribe started to become a civilization.

The heart of the essay was a description of a wood firing. The writer said, "Very few human events anymore bring people together this intensely for this long."

Except for birth, but the writer didn't say that. Instead he described the time the anonymous potter stored a pot in a river. When the potter pulled it out a year later, he found that he felt the way he had when he'd taken it warm from the kiln. The writer pointed out that the potter didn't have any kids.

I didn't mention any of this in the story I was writing. It shaped it the way a pot's defined by the empty space inside it.

After the story was published people said that writing it must have been difficult. It must've been hard, they said, to relive that. I said that it was. But it wasn't, not really. Not as hard as not writing it. As pretending that I wasn't reliving it anyway.

I finished writing the story nine months after the birthday, not that I noticed. I mailed it to my agent, who offered it to a magazine, who rejected it. A small magazine rejected it. A smaller one. A little one. On Bekah's birthday a man I'd never met in person read it, learned that no one else wanted it, and sent it to *The New Yorker.* They took it. Her story was over.

So I thought. The other thing that happened nine months after the birthday was a urine test. Bekah was pregnant.

A life after death; a real one, due nine months after our honeymoon. When I tried to imagine this baby it was faceless, not because its face was blank, but because I was afraid to look at it. But also because trying to picture my kid didn't feel like an act of imagination; it felt like a failure of my imagination. Like my mind knew that it was unequal to whatever could happen next.

Now that our first child had died, the odds of this one dying had doubled. If we lost this one, I could lose Bekah. I could see her not allowing me to sacrifice my life by giving it to someone who'd spend the rest of hers blaming herself.

My mind made me put the thought out of my mind. The worst that could happen had already happened.

When I told my dad that Bekah was pregnant he said, That's brave of her.

It was, but not to Bekah. Courage didn't feel brave. It felt like what had to be done. Like a job. Like work. When she wasn't working full-time at the office where she was only a name, she was driving across the city to ultrasounds, nonstress tests, and blood tests. To our endocrinologist, doctor, midwife, and doula. To a high-risk specialist who made her take a long needle full of blood thinner and inject it into her own belly twice a day, every day. She did all that, then the paperwork, then the insurance and reimbursement paperwork. She peeled, chopped, and cooked our vegetables. Took her thyroid pills. Made yogurt. Did yoga. Did everything. She didn't have time to be afraid.

But she was. In her seventh month she walked into the apartment, set down the bags she'd lugged up the stairs, and went into our bedroom. I was at the sink.

Hon?

Silence.

You okay?

A sniff.

I dried my hands and got on top of the bed with her. Spooned her.

Gestational diabetes, she said. Just like last time.

The nurse had talked to Bekah like Bekah had been pigging out on donuts and cookies. Like she hadn't done everything she was supposed to. Given her body everything. Her all. She had, and yet it was still failing her. Her own body.

We lay there for an hour, not moving. The school bell across the street rang. Kids shouted. Drivers honked. The warm air made our curtains breathe.

She said, This all makes me feel like I'm a vessel.

BUT that came later. In the beginning we agreed not to tell anyone that she was pregnant. That way we wouldn't have to tell anyone that the baby was dead.

At the twenty-week ultrasound a technician lubricated Bekah's belly and waved her plastic wand across it. The darkness on the screen contracted. Five faint white dots appeared. Fingertips. A raised hand. The darkness pulsed again. Two blind eyes emerged. A mouth opened.

I uttered a noise I can't re-create with words.

God, Bekah said.

A girl, the technician said.

BEFORE they published the story, the magazine paid me for it. This let me pay the rest of Irene's medical bills, which had continued to increase and multiply after she was dead. I sent money to a group of people like us, who didn't have a word to name them. Wine to the man who'd submitted the story to the magazine. For me, a 142-pound dictionary. Words were like species: They evolved, and I wanted the fossil record of that evolution, all 22,000 pages of it. Knowing what a word had meant could help me understand what it was now.

Here's one: *blessing*. From *blóedsian*, to stain with the blood of a sacrifice.

A week after Bekah's birthday a box came in the mail, addressed in a graceful, unfamiliar hand. It was the writer's, the one who'd written about pots. He'd sent us one of the anonymous potter's pots.

I'd told a faraway friend what the writer's essay had meant to me, and she'd asked him to send us one of the pots as a wedding present on her behalf. On their behalf; she and the writer were a couple now. When they got married a few years later we sent them one of Bekah's bowls, along with a card that said, "Long may you shape one another."

But that came later. The anonymous potter's pot was a sandy ochre jar with rusty strata, like an eroded riverbank. It looked like roots should be dangling from it. Inside it was still as smooth and pink as the day it was fired. Bekah and I kept our popcorn kernels in it. When the lid broke a couple years later I glued it back together. The repair was invisible from the outside; on the inside the break stood out like a crackle of lightning. I liked the jar even more this way, with a secret inside it.

My birthday was two weeks later. Bekah gave me a present I've forgotten, along with words I'll never forget:

You're not perfect, but you're perfect for me.

After that came Thanksgiving, and Christmas. The season. It started with a card that looked like an invitation to a wedding. But it was an invitation to a memorial service for dead babies. Bekah didn't want to go, but she agreed to go with me. The service was in the hospital where Irene was born. Rows of folding chairs led up to a podium and a table stocked with fruit juice and cookies.

I was there because I'd imagined communion. But the other parents weren't childless. A girl in a leopard skin tutu twirled her stuffed pink cat in my face. The boy behind us rocked back and forth in his chair; he wanted the juice and cookies *now.* Kids ran by squealing, banging into chairs. Now and then a mom or dad would snatch at a kid after it had ran past, but most of them sat dully, like they were waiting to see the doctor. One next to us nursed her newborn while her husband studied his hands.

A woman in high heels stood up and sang. As she sang she teetered down the aisle, seeking our eyes with hers. But most of the people spoke Spanish or Polish or Mandarin, so she sang alone. A pastor took the podium and read from a script. After she was done a translator leaned in. The microphone screeched. They wanted us to say, O God give us this, or O God grant us that, but no one was sure whether to say it in English or in Spanish, or after the English or after the Spanish, or both, or what. Babies cried.

I counted the pages left in the program.

This *is* going to be like a wedding.

I thought Bekah would smile a little, but she didn't. Something stopped her.

The pastor asked us to come up and share poetry or stories. Nobody moved.

I stood up and read a poem: "Despair." Bekah's best friend had sent it to us after the birthday. It was a good poem, but while I was reading it, the babies cried louder. Toddlers too. Nobody was despairing the way I'd thought they would.

The moms and dads who went up to the podium after me choked on their own words. You didn't need to understand their language to know what they were saying.

We ended in a circle. A mom said the name of her child and lit the candle of the mom next to her. Around we went, including Irene, until the flame circled back to the altar. The pastor thumbed a button on a boom box: another hymn. No one sang. The crying was a cacophony. When the hymn ended we lowered our heads and blew out the candles. At last. The pastor gestured toward the juice and cookies. The kids shrieked and ran up front and devoured them.

In the parking lot Bekah took my hand. She squeezed it.

I'm so glad I didn't know how awful that would be. If I'd known, I wouldn't've come. I'd have missed it.

Kids, I said. They ruined it, but they also kind of saved it.

The next party was at a friend's; his Christmas combined with her Chanukah. The biology teacher came with her nine-month-old. We took her baby out of her sling and passed her around. After Bekah had had her turn she said, I'm going to have a baby.

I wasn't surprised that she'd said it; I was surprised that it sounded true.

Get over here, the biology teacher cried. She gathered Bekah into her arms and planted her head on Bekah's shoulder, grafting it there. She stroked and patted her back.

You too.

She waved me over. I put down my plate and wrapped my arms around them. The biology teacher looked up at the party.

I'm sorry, she said.

She sniffed, closed her eyes, shook her head. Denied what she said even as she said it again:

I'm sorry.

IRENE's birthday drew near. I didn't think of it as her first, but her second. I had to count the day itself. The zero. First came the eve of Christmas Eve, when I'd shrugged at what must have been her death throes. Bekah and I got on a flight to Texas. As we flew over the Lake I thought about pouring Irene's ashes into it. About the fact that she'd lived and died underwater, in the pond inside her mom. The rhyme attracted me. But Bekah had borne her, not me. She'd decide what to do with her.

I don't remember what my mom gave us for Christmas, or what we gave her. Or each other. I remember the walk we took through dry woods. We ate lunch on the side of a hill, beneath a mesquite. Then we lay down in the sun. Birds sang. A squirrel rustled. The stillness overcame us. When I woke up I thought, That was happiness, right there: being dissolved into something complete and great.

Before we flew back to Chicago we took a walk around a lake, killing time.

What are you going to do when you get back, my mom said.

I don't know, I said. Christmas'll always be . . .

I held up my empty hands.

My mom twirled her thumbs, tracing the loops of the invisible cursive she writes in while she's thinking, the way another woman's lips might count while her fingers knit.

I had a stillborn sister, she said.

I knew it, I thought. I hadn't known, but I should've.

Bekah said, Was she older than you or younger than you?

Older. She would've been older.

Then my mom said her sister's name:

Heather. Heather Kimble.

She walked on, her head inclined to one side, resisting an extradimensional voice, or leaning toward another. Her thumbs kept writing something that vanished the moment it existed.

I'd met the woman who'd borne this dead baby, but

only a few times, each time for less than a day. Granny was deaf and foreign. She didn't speak. Grampy did the talking. The only real communication Granny and I had had was an aerogramme she'd mailed me after Irene's birthday. Thin blue whorls on blue tissue: the hand of a stranger. The letter didn't mention stillbirth. It begged me to leave everything to the keeper of the world before and after this one. Trust God, the script said. God, God, God, as though the word could cover up a name she couldn't bear to write, let alone speak: Heather. Heather Kimble.

I'd thrown out the letter. On the flight back to Chicago I started to regret this; to miss an ancestor I'd never really known, and one I'd never known about. My mom had given me something I'd never forget.

When we got back to our place Bekah and I slid into bed and each other. I tried not to think about what else was inside her. I could feel its movements mingling with my own. I almost had to stop.

In the morning I handed Bekah a present: a book about the Great Plains. She looked down at it.

It's Irene's birthday, I said.

Oh.

She'd forgot.

But she hadn't, not really. For three hundred and

sixty-four days straight she'd thought about the birthday. Today was no different.

Neither of us cried. I felt like I owed it to Irene, but no tears came. No words either. Our thoughts were too big for us. We went shopping for a present for the cartoonist's birthday party. The biology teacher opened their door.

You do not have to be here, she said. But I'm glad you are.

I handed her the present, which I've forgotten. I can't forget the present I gave her at that same birthday party three years later: a book for her, as a token of the season. Before I wrapped the book I did something I'd never done with a present: I read it, holding it by its edges so I wouldn't leave a trace.

The book was about cells. The writer had started as one. Before that he'd been a half life, one split between his mom's egg and his dad's sperm. When those halves met and married he became the cell that reenacted our evolution. He split into two, four, eight, morphing into something like a tadpole. His gills became lungs, his dorsal fin a spine, his fins flippers, then limbs. Morphogenesis: the only miracle. It can't happen without death. Billions of cells have to die for an embryo to become a fetus, billions more for the fetus to become a baby.

The writer said, "By the time I was born, more of me had died than survived."

That sentence gave me something. But what? I knew that Irene's death was random. Chance killed her, just like it kills the two and a half million babies born dead every year. I could accept this, but I'd be damned if I could bring myself to believe in it.

Maybe I could, if we all die before we're born.

The story was still at the magazine. Still gestating. Nine months went by between the day they accepted it and the day they published it. From a distance it would look like anyone else's story: a chain of twenty-six letters, ten digits, a handful of punctuation marks. A strand, uniform but unique, that could encode endless information. Typeset, the strand would only be six pages long. But it would have a header, footers, a spine. My body of work. I daydreamed about holding it.

At the end of the year the magazine sent a photographer to our apartment. When she walked in and saw Bekah pregnant, her brown eyes got wet. We closed ours and the camera in the palm of her hand clicked.

She mailed us the photograph. My profile in front of Bekah's face, merging into a single, misshapen face split down its middle. Our closed eyes made it seem as though what had made us merge had also made us shy. What had fused us also separated us. But it wasn't a portrait of us; the subject of the photo was Irene. We hung it over our bed.

The university down the street needed someone to teach people how to tell true stories. I'd never taught before but I applied, using the embryo as my writing sample. I got the job. A teacher, like my dad. I'd have the first steady paycheck I'd had in eleven years, and something I'd almost never had, not since college: health insurance. Bekah quit the office where she was only a name. She couldn't bear the thought of trying to raise a child with the amount of stress she'd been under. Now she didn't have to; all she had to bear was her child.

When I called my mom to tell her the news, she said something almost no one says: my daughter's name.

Oh Dan. Irene gave you so much.

I didn't say anything. Her death wasn't a gift. But it had been given to me. I'd had to take it. Maybe taking it was making the worst thing that had ever happened to me seem like the greatest thing. Not the best thing, the biggest thing. The awesome thing, in the old sense of the word, the sense that's almost as dead as Irene. I didn't trust anyone to understand this. I didn't understand it myself. It took me years to stop being mad at my mom for saying it.

Three weeks before the baby was due, the story went to the printer. It's done, I thought: Good night, Irene. I'd thought her name a thousand times, but this was the first time I'd pretended I was saying it to her, not to myself, or to some imaginary reader.

After the story was published, ones like it came in the mail. One man wrote to say that his daughter had been born alive. He'd held her and watched the doctor who'd just delivered her hack open her mom's rib cage and reach into her chest and beat her heart with his hands, hoping that it would start beating again on its own. It didn't. He and his daughter went home alone.

A woman said she'd given birth twenty-eight years ago, during a blizzard. She and her husband had never spoken of that night. Until now. She wanted me to know that, and the one thing she remembered about their son:

He had red hair.

Irene's birthday present came. A baby blanket, woven by my twin's girlfriend. She'd stopped weaving after the birthday, but the thought of giving it had proved less excruciating than leaving it undone, so she'd woven Irene's name and birth date into it, along with the words, *In Loving Memory.* I lifted it to my face and inhaled. Lamb's wool: like straw, with a hint of the barnyard. Of manure. Bekah draped the blanket across the backrest of our couch. A few weeks later I noticed that the blanket was gone. I found it in the closet. Then on our bed. Back in the living room. In another closet.

Then the half room, the room that didn't really have a name. Where we put everything we didn't use, but couldn't bring ourselves to give away. The blanket was something we couldn't hide, but couldn't display. We had nowhere to put it.

A cup came in the mail. It was small and green with wavy sides, as though the potter had scooped up pond water and swirled it. No initials, no insignia. A nameless return address. An illegible signature on the postcard at the bottom of the packing peanuts. I turned over the card. A photo of a pot I'd never seen. But I recognized it.

On the Valentine's Day trip to my dad's I'd gone down to his basement, where I'd stored the relics of my childhood: damp, spotted horror comics, war comics, and army fatigues. A rusty toy rifle. Letters in girlish hands, references to pregnancy scares I'd thought I'd never forget. I threw them out. I threw out the short stories I'd written in college. My art portfolio. The only pot I'd ever made. It was a thick oval vase I'd built in college. I'd been smoothing its flanks with slip when my teacher had said, I think that pot's trying to become a fish.

She was right. It looked like a carp with its mouth open. I ruined it by adding eyes, scales, barbels. By trying to make it actually look like a carp with its mouth open. Trying to make it realistic made it look fake. I dropped it into my dad's garbage can.

The pot on the postcard was also a carp. Sort of. Instead of scales this one had the rusty reflections scales would've made. Seashells pressed into it gave the impression of fins. Unlike me, this potter had left room for the imagination. He'd given it life.

Who was he? Or she? Not the first anonymous potter; that one lived out West. The return address on this one was from the East. I typed it into a search engine and found it paired with an email address. I emailed a thank-you note. Seven days later a poem came back. The potter had written it about the day his son was born, when the hospital had made him wait alone outside the delivery room.

"They both happen behind the scenes," he said: "This making of the one from two and the two from one."

At the end of his letter was a quote he attributed to Willa Cather:

"The artist loves the things that haunt him."

RIGHT about this time, the fetus turned head over heels. In the breech, like her sister. Bekah tried massage, acupuncture, yoga, but the baby wouldn't turn back around. She couldn't be born, only delivered.

The morning of the cesarean the sky was purple. Bekah's belly was as hard as a farm egg. I was buckling our empty safety seat into our car when a man in oily clothing marched toward us, singing the theme song to a movie about prisoners of war. The local legend about this guy was that a long time ago he'd accidentally killed his wife and kids in a car crash. He held up a playing card to block Bekah from his sight.

Dirty whore! Filthy whore!

We got in our car and pulled out into traffic.

Cowards!

At the stop sign the long white convertible behind us honked. I turned around in my seat, picturing an old man in a tracksuit and gold jewelry behind the wheel. That's what the driver was wearing, but he didn't look old enough to drive. Neither did his passengers. Their stereo pounded like a heartbeat as they drove around us and ran the stop sign.

Lake Shore Drive was lined with cop cars. Choppers chopped overhead. Riot squads clopped by on horseback. The President was in town to give a speech declaring progress in the war he'd already declared over and won. The war in the birthplace of civilization. He was giving the speech to a group of people who owned restaurants.

What kind of world are we bringing you into?

I didn't say this out loud. I said it to myself. It was the first thing I said to Irene's sister.

The Lake was as blue as the sky. Green leaves gleamed along the shore. After we passed the canyons of downtown I pulled over and parked.

Our last walk as a couple, I said.

Bekah slipped off her sandals. We passed scorched driftwood, a lone, upright beer bottle in the sand. Closer to shore, sea glass and shells. Moms pushing strollers covered in the emblazonry of mountain-climbing gear. The birthday seemed even more unimaginable than it had when it had felt like a failure to try to imagine it.

I can't believe it, we said. It doesn't seem real.

At the hospital we passed the room where a stranger named Irene had laid her palm against her chest. The one where I'd read "Despair." One where our doctor had stripped the slick glove from her hand and said, I think that's it. The hospital didn't assign us that room; they gave us one that was its mirror image. Bekah asked me if being in it gave me flashbacks. I didn't answer. It wasn't a question.

A baby's heartbeat sounded through the wall; it sounded like I was under water, hearing a basketball being bounced.

A nurse attached Bekah to a machine and a ribbon of graph paper oozed out of it, marking the range of Bekah's second heartbeat. One that sounded like another basketball being bounced.

Is this your first pregnancy?

Fourth.

And what were the results of the other three?

Termination. Then miscarriage. Then stillbirth.

I couldn't help remembering that a row of tombstones is called a plotline.

Did we have a pediatrician picked out?

We didn't. We hadn't assumed anything. Assuming could cause the same thing that happened last time to happen this time.

The nurse slipped a needle into Bekah's arm. Attendants handed her waivers. Sign here, here, here, and here.

The doctor who'd delivered Irene walked in. Our doctor.

At last, she said.

I said, There's no one we'd rather have deliver our girl today.

A knot of figures surrounded Bekah, dressed like followers of an otherworldly faith. Nothing showed but their eyes. They shaved her, swabbed her, drugged her. I imagined them reaching into her and pulling out a girl who'd kick the way Irene had kicked at the end. Before I could say goodbye, they wheeled Bekah out the door. I was alone on a wrinkled bed. I was thirty-seven and a half years old; chances were, my life was half over. I stepped into my paper suit. The puffy cap and shoe covers made me feel like a giant toddler.

A nurse led me into the operating room. I sat next to Bekah and took her cold hand in mine. We didn't speak. Whatever happened next would remarry us.

The blue screen across Bekah's torso stopped me from seeing inside her. Drops of blood freckled it. I looked away. A stainless steel cart loaded with oxygen canisters. Next to the canisters, Bekah's sandals, tucked against each other.

Stand up, dad.

I stood up. An upside-down baby, as blue as a blueberry, dripping.

Look at that pout.

I looked. I saw Irene. I remembered her. Then someone snipped the umbilical cord and the memory was gone; only the thought of it was left. The baby spluttered and choked and turned pink. An internal organ became a human being. She cried. Then I cried.

"That is happiness," Willa Cather wrote: "to be dissolved into something complete and great."

I'd read this sentence fifteen years ago and didn't realize that I'd memorized it until the day I'd poured Irene's ashes into her urn, when it had come back to me. It had come back again on her birthday, and now on her sister's birthday.

We named her sister Willa.

Bekah told me that every time she left Willa alone, even for a minute, she was sure that when she got back, she'd find her dead. I thought so too. So did Willa. When mom left the room, she'd left forever. Willa grieved and grieved.

I didn't; it was more subtle than that. Like when I saw the nurse put Willa under the heat lamp. When her first black turd slithered out of her butt. When Bekah's sister walked her around the room, rocking her. Singing to her. When Bekah's aunts came bearing presents. When I woke up to crying in the middle of the night. It wasn't until the day after the birthday, right before the milk and eggs and another social worker, that I woke up and saw Willa asleep, her hair dry, her face already plumper and younger-looking, and realized that it hadn't been a dream. My girl was alive.

I cupped her head in my hands. The cracks in it had made her human. They let our brains grow inside mom, but squeeze through the birth canal without killing us both. They let it grow three times bigger in our first year, the expansion that makes us helpless the longest, but eventually the strongest. The most powerful. That helplessness is what makes us us; is that why we can't really remember it? Or ever really forget it? Mine was still a part of me in ways I could recognize, but never understand. Life felt like following a maze, the maze of the personality impressed on me by everything I'd never remember.

Willa's eyes were blue. By the end of the year they'd be green and brown at once. Olive or hazel, depending on the light. A year after that one started drifting in and out of alignment, making her look cross-eyed. When that happened, something impossible happened: I loved her even more.

Now she kept her eyes shut, like oysters. She preferred the world she'd come from. She seemed more human in it. Asleep she'd yawn, mewl, relax. Show concern, distaste, outrage. Then peace. We huddled around her like she was a campfire, watching her shift and sigh and settle into sleep. In her face I saw flickers of me and Bekah. Of my mom and dad, Bekah's mom and dad. Relatives. Ancestors. People I'd never seen, and couldn't recognize.

Around midnight I passed the nursery window: a dozen newborns swaddled in pink-and-blue blankets, capped by pink-and-blue beanies. They looked jaundiced and ancient. As alike as larvae. Any one of them could've been mine. I wanted to hold them all.

I was bringing our empty safety seat up on the elevator when a stranger got on and smiled.

First one?

Years later Willa asked me why I wore a ring.

Because I'm married, I said. To Mom.

No. Why is it a *ring*?

Because. After we had Willa Bekah and I did the same things in the same order, every day. The bus to my office, the students an incarnation of the ones I'd had last time. The bus home, the cups and plates I'd washed and dried that morning. After dinner bath, book, bedtime. Then our bedtime. Weekends, laundry. If it wasn't raining I'd call up the painter and we'd pedal his twins and Willa along the Lake. I lived for that. Cycling was our break from the cycle. Once a week Bekah and I'd make love. Once a month we'd argue, always about the same things: a cycle we recognized, but couldn't understand. Holidays we went back to where we'd lived as kids, where we saw the people we'd been kids with. We talked about our kids and how they did so many of the things we'd done.

The beginning of Willa's childhood, and the end of mine. Days, weeks, months. Years. Every day ended with the most inscribed, sacred circle of all: one of us walking around and around our kitchen with Willa against our chest, lulling her to sleep. Like a dog who has to turn around and around before she lays herself down. Like life wasn't a route, but a rut. What shaped us, instead of us shaping it. At the center of every one of those turns was our kitchen table, and the bowl Bekah gave me for our first Christmas.

For Willa's first Christmas Bekah's grandpa flew the three of us to his retirement villa in the desert. The pot in Poppa's casita looked familiar, but it was more bulbous than the ones at our place. More pregnant. This happened whenever we visited Bekah's friends and family. She'd given away her best pots.

After the big day and the adoration of Willa I flew back to Chicago alone, to get my classes ready. I didn't get anything ready. I spent Irene's birthday thinking that it was her second, but also her third. I didn't know what to think. So I did something with my hands.

I threw out my collection of hot sauce bottles, which had looked like toy soldiers on top of our kitchen cabinets. I dug in the cabinets for Bekah's pots. The runts of the litters. I knew that now. I lined them up where the soldiers had been. I hung her plates like paintings, along with a couple of serving trays that had been a present. I took six sake cups we'd been given at our wedding and set them like stones along a long, thin shelf. There. Now the collection was about pots, not just her pots. Now she couldn't accuse me of showing her off.

When she and Willa got back from the desert she

stopped in the kitchen door. She looked at me like I'd hung up a dozen pictures of her when she was young. Of her former selves.

Look at what you did.

Actually, I said, you did it.

Irene's urn was up there too. I'd thought about cracking it open and planting it like a seed. About roots drawing her ashes up into leaves that would turn the color of flame. But we didn't own any land to plant a tree in. All we had was this apartment. This box.

After we got Willa to sleep in her crib we made love. When we were finished Willa woke up. Grieving again. The only way to stop her grief was to burp her. To change her, feed her, hold her. Rock her. Walk her. To do everything for her.

I lifted her out of her crib and tucked her in between us. She snuggled where I'd snuggled and sucked where I'd sucked. She smacked her lips and sighed, breathing in the warm, breadlike smell of us. Bekah caressed her the way she'd caressed me a minute ago, moving from loving me to loving her so seamlessly, so innocently that I got scared. We'd been lovers. This was like being family.

Four

I CAN'T REMEMBER WHEN WE MADE OUR NEXT ONE. Probably on Father's Day. Ten weeks after Father's Day was our ten-week ultrasound. I also don't remember Bekah telling me that she was pregnant again. I've forgotten the big events: Willa's first smile, first word, first step. The first time she called me Dad. So many moments; their momentousness overwhelmed the moments themselves, right when my memory of them was forming, or should've formed.

Maybe that's why Willa can't remember her infancy either. It erases itself. Giving birth must work the same way. That must be why Bekah could do it, and still choose to do it again.

Also because she'd been one of five kids, raised by a woman who'd told us, It doesn't even start to feel like a family until you've had your third.

Why did I want another kid? Because I didn't. Willa

was my everything. When I took her to the park she pointed and said, Dis.

Squirrel, I said. Pigeon. Crow.

She pointed at every living thing while I shuffled behind her, stooped over so I could hold onto her hand.

That's all I wanted, right there. But Willa was what I hadn't wanted. What I'd once said I never wanted. Not until Irene.

How had Willa lived? Right where Irene had died?

WEIRD.

That's the first word our doctor said after she'd finished examining Bekah's uterus. This was a few weeks after Willa was born. Using the ultrasound as a monitor, she'd seen an anomaly. A dark spot. When she tried to zoom in on it, it disappeared.

You may need a specialist.

We'd already seen one. A high-risk one, after Irene. He'd studied his clipboard and said, Preexisting conditions?

I told him about Bekah's thyroid.

No relation. Family history?

Bekah said, My brother died when he was four.

I'd seen this brother. There was a photo of him stuck to

Bekah's mom's refrigerator: baseball hat, a fishing pole. I'd also seen the photo at Bekah's dad's house, twelve hundred miles away. He had a copy of it stuck to his refrigerator.

The boy Bekah had spoken of, but never really talked about: She wound up telling me about him one night at our kitchen table, when Willa was nine months old.

He'd been the four sisters' baby too. The baby of the family. Its nucleus. Everything revolved around him.

I asked her what they did when he died.

Nothing.

She was seventeen; he was four. His lips were blue. He was sick, but he'd been sick since the day he was born. He'd had surgery before, and he'd lived. He'd always lived. When her mom and dad drove him to Springfield for another operation, Bekah's sisters threw a party. Cigarettes, beer foam on the ceiling. Bekah's memory didn't admit anything after that. The next day she was down in a boy's basement, making out with him, when the phone rang.

For you, Bekah.

She picked up the receiver.

Come home. Click.

Bekah hoped that the party was the trouble, but when she saw her mom and dad's car in the driveway, days before they were supposed to be back, she knew.

Her mom lay in bed with her back to the door. She didn't speak, even when they asked her to.

At school one of Bekah's teachers pulled her aside.

You know you don't have to be here.

Bekah told him that she wanted to.

Her mom got out of bed in time to sew the dress that Bekah wore to her high school graduation. When Bekah came back nine months later for spring break, her dad was drinking a beer at the kitchen table. For breakfast.

Your mother's asked me to move out.

In the next few years the middle sisters dropped out of school. One wound up following a group that called itself The Dead; the other moved away with a girl who turned up dead, years later. The youngest shaved her head.

Wait.

Bekah was staring into the corner of our kitchen. They hadn't done nothing when her brother died. She remembered people in their living room. They'd made a circle and taken turns saying what they remembered about their baby. Bekah remembered what she said. What she'd remembered. But she didn't tell me. She never has.

How do I mourn someone I never knew? And was that someone Bekah's brother, or Bekah?

Bekah told the specialist that her brother had been born with a faulty heart valve. No reason, not that anyone could find. The specialist prescribed the blood thinner that she'd had to inject twice a day.

My new job came with new insurance, who assigned us a new doctor and a new specialist, one in assisted reproductive technology, ART.

I told him, There's a mystery spot.

He said, There's always a mystery spot.

Bekah's uterus was split down the middle. Her grandfather had called it heart-shaped; the specialist said that it was either septate, divided into two separate chambers, or bicornuate, split into two horns.

The MRI was inconclusive, but it did find the mystery spot. Decidua, the specialist called it: matter from a previous pregnancy. Usually the mother reincorporates the remains; these were like a fossil. Removing them might help the next placenta attach to the uterine wall, but it also might not. It might mar the uterus more than the remains themselves. There was no way to know until after the operation, when it couldn't be undone. That's why the specialist couldn't make the decision. Bekah had to.

Take it out, she said.

Afterward the specialist said, It wasn't easy. But we got it out of there.

The dark matter, I said.

No, Bekah said. White matter.

The specialist nodded. A calcified uterine mass.

A couple weeks after the operation I moved Irene's ashes from the kitchen into our room, above Bekah's side of the bed. There. Now she was where we'd made her. I'd done something for her.

I TOLD my students that the secret to writing about their own lives was that it wasn't about them. It was about their reader. I said, Think about this person you're writing to, or for. Who is she? Someone you're close to; someone you can tell anything to. And that's because you don't know her. She's your familiar, but she's a total stranger.

Some of my students had fought in Iraq. They hadn't won the war; war had won the war. Now that they were home, this victory was becoming clear. The Corpsman's flattop made him look like he came from the time when our parents were kids. He'd reenlisted after September 11th. He was a medic; he wanted to save lives. He came back wanting to take them. Whose I could never tell. His superiors at the infamous prison. The prisoners he'd also grown to hate. The enemy he'd never even seen.

A concentration camp, he said. We ran a concentration camp.

The Lieutenant had run a rifle company. His job had

been to keep men who were really boys alive. He'd done it, but not perfectly. Nobody could've. His boys had killed the enemy, but also each other. Fratricide, he called it: accidents. But the accidents didn't stop when the combat stopped. The war went on. His boys who weren't boys anymore went back to lives that didn't feel like theirs anymore. One night two of them were arguing, a loaded handgun between them. Playing around, the one who survived called it. The Lieutenant didn't talk about it; I think that's why he was writing about it.

As far as I could tell the worst part of combat hadn't been the fear of being killed; it had been the fear of getting the guy next to them killed. Of losing someone else's life. The moment these soldiers wanted to forget, but always remember, was when they'd held their dead. Someone was a body. Now that someone felt even more like family.

Irene had died fighting. This didn't change anything, but it was all I had, so I took a grim pride in it, and in her. And in my wife. She volunteered to deliver Irene, and until not long ago a woman who went into labor was as likely to die as a guy who went into battle. More likely: During World War I, more Americans died in childbirth than on the battlefield. That's why tribes initiate their boys around the time girls get their first period. Guys need to prove that they can face death the way women have to. The way

Bekah did. She's the woman who showed me how to be a man.

I had another thing in common with these veterans: the word *infantry*. I dug up the origin in my dictionary: foot soldiers with small arms. Also babies as a whole. Infants as a body. That last meaning was archaic; you could only use it as a joke.

One student wanted to write about someone she'd met only once, but couldn't forget.

That's a good one, I said. That's one I ought to do myself.

She'd met the one she couldn't forget at a party. She'd never seen him before, but she knew who he was. Everyone did. He was the most popular kid on the island. Also the only black kid on the island.

The nicest guy in the world, she said. That's what everyone said. They were right.

He'd come from the mainland. Away, as the islanders called it. His foster parents on the island hadn't really wanted him either. They'd kicked him out after the checks stopped coming, on his eighteenth birthday. So the island adopted him. Gave him old clothes, odd jobs, couches to crash on. Elected him prom king. Some people said he was retarded but he wasn't. He'd developed cerebral palsy or something and it was starting to retard his speech a little.

There was something so pure about him, she told me. You wanted to curl up in his lap.

So she did. She said that he'd almost died of embarrassment.

Later that summer he did die.

An accident, the islanders told her. One they didn't want to talk about.

She asked a summer kid.

It wasn't an accident, he said. Even I know that.

Everyone knew that the kid was afraid of the water. He couldn't swim. So why would he leave a party one night and get in a boat without wearing a life jacket? With a guy who'd been telling anyone who'd listen that he wanted to kill black people? Who'd already done time down in Florida for murder?

Maybe because at the party this guy and the kid had had words, which had ended with the guy saying that things were now settled between them. They were cool. To prove it, they should get in that skiff right now and fish. The stripers were running. People at the party could hear the two out on the water, arguing again. They heard one of them cry, Help. A rescue party found the guy hanging on to the boat; they found the kid at the bottom of the harbor. His body was naked.

The guy said it was an accident. The police reported it as one. So did the coroner. The newspaper. But if it was an accident, it was an accident that was meant to happen. An accident someone had planned. People knew. One morning the guy noticed a bullet hole in the driver's side door of his car. He got in and left the island. He didn't come back. He went back to where he'd also come from: away. Flowers appeared along the causeway, next to graffiti that said, *Rest In Peace.*

The island mentality, I said. That's the story. That's what killed the kid, and that's why they let this guy get away with it. With murder. If that's really what this is. If this story you're telling is actually true.

Why did I want it to be true? So that a kid wouldn't die by accident?

You've got to go back there, I said. Find someone who'll talk.

She didn't think she had the right. It wasn't her story.

In the scene where you sit in his lap, you need to bring him to life. You need details. Make him live on the page.

I can't. It was a party. I was drunk.

She'd never forget him, but she couldn't really remember him.

I went to the library and dug up the kid's death certificate. His basketball scores. His yearbook photo. This is it, I thought. I'll fly to the coast, rent a car, and tell the islanders that I'm writing a tribute to the most popular kid on their island. It's true, the half of the truth that'll lead me to someone who'll break the silence. Who'll give me the reason he died.

Bekah would have her own reasons for coming. The island was the one where potters gathered, where she'd sold her big pot. That auction had been the beginning of the end of something. By going back to where that end began, she'd start over. We both would.

But I was forgetting something: Willa. She had to have checkups. Tests, shots, eyeglasses. Insurance. I couldn't go back to freelancing. I went back to my classroom and told myself that I wasn't a quitter. I wasn't a dad who abandoned my kid. I was a dad who abandoned someone else's kid.

My student took another stab at the story, but her telling of it got worse. I gave it back to her covered in red.

It's your baby, I said. Not mine.

THAT's what I did for a job. A living. The other half of my living was a book I was supposed to write, one I'd had all planned when Irene died. It was about comic books. The man who'd fathered them almost two hundred years ago had called them his problem child. That's because pirates had copied them, and the copies had spawned copies of the copies, until people forgot the father. I wrote about that and three cartoonists I knew. The first was the one who had the same birthday as Irene; he'd written a book about a boy looking for the dad he'd never known. The second cartoonist had written a book about a boy looking for the dad *he'd* never known. The third cartoonist was a father figure to the first two; he'd also written a book about his dad, a man he'd always known, but never understood.

When my classes let out for the summer I checked into a cabin in the mountains, where I tried to resuscitate the book. I started by remembering the comics I'd made in sixth grade. I'd slaved over their covers, then left the insides blank. Then I burned them. I'd also built model tanks and plastic soldiers. I burned these too; not realistic enough. In college I'd written fiction. One story was about a boy who couldn't speak; the other was about a writer who couldn't write. The writer was stuck inside a cabin in the mountains.

Everything I'd ever done was stillborn; everything but my story about my stillborn. I knew this, but I kept on believing in my book. My notes for it piled up like leaves under a tree.

One day my cell phone rang.

Guess what.

She'd been in the car with Willa, buckled up and waiting to take a left turn, when some lady in a gigantic SUV who was digging in her purse drove through the intersection and Bang!

I screamed, Bekah said. Willa didn't start screaming until later, after it was over.

Is—

She's fine. We're both fine. Both totally unhurt. She's sleeping in my arms.

The car was totaled. They were sitting next to it and the groceries that had been in the trunk. I was walking barefoot up the trail. I had no memory of leaving the cabin. When Bekah and Willa pulled up a week later in our new used car, I held them like they were something I could absorb.

That was in August. On Halloween we went to the biology teacher's party. When we were leaving the cartoonist said, Wait: I forgot to give you something.

He left the room and came back with a copy of his new book. This took a few seconds.

We buckled Willa into the car and got on the freeway.

A man who didn't want to live anymore drove toward us, hoping to hit someone head on. We never saw him coming. A flash. Smoke exploded in front of us as Bekah braked to a stop. The car two cars in front of us was a tower of flame; the family of four inside it was turning to ash. The suicide's car looked like a cigarette that had been stubbed out. It steamed in our headlights.

The driver behind us honked and flashed his brights. He rolled down his window. So did Bekah. He stuck out his fist, then his middle finger as he pulled around us and sped off, the flanks of his taxi shining in the firelight.

Hook-and-ladders roared in, whining and blatting. A firefighter jumped out: Stay in your car! He walked over to the stubbed-out car and said something. Whoever was inside must've answered, because a half dozen firefighters rushed over and started yanking at the door.

Oh no, Bekah said. I can't look.

But she did. So did I. Willa tried to, but from her safety seat in the back she couldn't see what was happening, only what was happening to our faces.

A firefighter staggered back, hugging the door. The others swarmed in. The woman in the car in front of us got out from behind the wheel, flipped open her cell phone, and raised it to the scene. In it, tiny firefighters swarmed a tiny wreck.

Oh God, Bekah said. I can't believe this is happening. I can't believe she's filming this. No.

A guy smoking a cig walked up and flipped open his own phone. The two of them talked and smoked like they were staring into a campfire.

Is that what I was doing? Not with a phone, but with words.

BEFORE Willa was born I'd thought that if we could just get her to zero and alive, my worries would be over. But as soon as I strapped her into her safety seat to drive her home from the hospital, I knew I had worry.

When she didn't crawl when she was supposed to. When she broke out in a rash. When her eye crossed. Whenever we went anywhere on my bike. I had to thread the needle through thickets of cars, buses, and trucks. On our way to meet up with the painter one day we passed the court by the Lake, the one where Irene had almost died before she died. Where were those kids now?

In Iowa City my twin and I had walked our newspaper routes alone in the dark. We threw our bikes down in our front yard and slept with our doors unlocked. We were afraid of a couple older kids, but our parents weren't. Why would they? Back then, kids weren't the most dangerous thing.

When a teaching job opened up in Iowa City I applied, using the embryo as my writing sample. They scheduled my interview for the day after Irene's birthday.

Christmas morning I woke up before dawn and drove to my dad's house, through fields whose furrows were like the whorls of an enormous thumbprint. Past the pillar of fire and Peace Road. We were met at the door and served coffee, bacon, and orange juice. The hissing fire, the crackling presents. The phone calls. We woke up the next day in my old bedroom. Time to go: The interview was back in Chicago, on account of all the other applicants flying in. As we crossed the river and the spot where I'd kneeled before our dark taillight, I had the sense that that past wasn't past, and was still about to rear-end us.

I spent Irene's birthday looking at the questions that I'd be asked at tomorrow's interview. Essay questions. Instead of thinking about them, I thought about the person I'd never remember, and never forget. The next morning I walked into a room full of strangers and forgot things almost as soon as I'd said them. I walked out knowing I'd blown it.

I hadn't wanted the job on the day it counted most. It had felt wrong to want anything on Irene's birthday. The only thing that didn't feel wrong was not moving and not talking. Not really thinking, either. It felt right to be still, and be. To be aware of myself as a being.

Is that a Sabbath?

After Father's Day it got hard not to tell people that Bekah was pregnant again. Especially our matchmakers, at their tenth wedding anniversary. A party, with beer and a band in their backyard. The next day I put Willa on my bike and rode her to the zoo, where we petted goats and their kids. On the way back to our place the rhythm of the road under our wheels lulled Willa and she slumped forward in her seat, asleep. We were passing a spot I'd passed a thousand times before when I noticed a brown-and-gold historical marker that hadn't been there. I stopped and went back. The marker said, *Hidden Truths.*

More than fifteen thousand people had been buried here, some in a row with headstones, some jumbled together in trenches. Some at night when no one was looking. Now it was a softball diamond, but it had been a mass grave for Indians, indigents, infants. Jews. This was the potter's field.

That name: It comes from the story of the boy born on the day Irene died, who almost died on the day she was born. December 28th is the Massacre of the Innocents, when the King murdered every newborn in Bethlehem.

The one he was after escaped and grew up to be the man who was sacrificed after his friend Judas sold him out for thirty pieces of silver. Priests used the silver to buy the field where potters dug their clay. From now on that's where they'd bury everyone who had no one.

I walked Willa along the sidelines to the beach, where I laid her down in the lacy shade of a locust tree. She rolled onto her back, her hands up by her ears, her head to one side, like she'd been shot while surrendering. A fly landed on her dress. Another crawled up her leg. Dead to the world: The phrase came against my will. Willa's chest rose and fell, the skyscrapers behind her like gigantic crystals formed by the Lake's evaporation, their antennae tuned to a world beyond this one.

Chicago. It was glass, steel, and stone. Mineral. It wasn't alive. But it wasn't dead. By living in it, we haunted it. We gave it something like a life.

I remembered a time I'd been in the half room, trying to remember what it was I'd come in there to look for, when a red balloon blew past the window, trailing a cord. I'd stood at the window and watched the balloon wave higher and higher, in and out of clouds until it was gone.

I wanted to release Irene's ashes into the air. Into the Lake. In the field where everyone who didn't belong belonged.

Just last week I'd noticed Willa standing on top of Bekah's bedside table, reaching for Irene's urn. I'd snatched her up and carried her out of the room. I don't know what I was more scared of: her breaking the urn, or her asking me what was in it.

BEKAH called me after the ten-week ultrasound. Could I leave work early and relieve the babysitter?

Sure. How'd it go?

There was no heartbeat.

Heels clacking in a corridor. A loudspeaker parroting the name of an absent doctor.

I can't talk about it.

Neither could I. I said something I'll never remember and pedaled back to our apartment, past babies set like jewels in the hollows of their strollers. The first cold air in months blew in from the Lake. I put on a sweater and stood on the back porch with Willa, hugging her, feeling small compared to my thoughts.

Bekah called again. Could I get a bottle of wine?

She was calm when she came into the kitchen. After we ate and got Willa bathed and in bed and asleep we sat on the back porch with our twin glasses of red.

The new doctor had said, No heartbeat. Hm. This has happened before? You had a stillbirth? For no apparent reason? He'd excused himself. He never came back.

I cursed his name.

The technicians had taken an interest. One had said, There's something else in there. A spot.

I thought the specialist removed that, I said.

No, Bekah said. That was white matter.

I didn't ask any more questions. My job tonight was to listen.

While she'd waited for the doctor to never come back, Bekah'd reread the emails she'd sent after Irene. She was surprised at how philosophical she'd been. How composed. How she'd said that good things had come of it too.

Of course that was two weeks after it happened, she said. Later I lost it.

She wished we had our old doctor back. At this new hospital she was just a name. A case, with no case history. She hated the loss of that history. Having to explain everything all over again to every white coat who walked into the room. Saying the same things over and over felt like the reason the same things kept happening.

After her second glass of wine she told me about the garden she'd had before she met me. She'd had so many tomatoes that at this point every summer she'd throw away the more imperfect ones. Ones that had split or gone soft. She'd chuck them into a compost heap. One night she missed the heap and the tomato smacked against the house next door, where there was a party. She ran upstairs and locked her door, afraid a partier would be outraged by the overripe tomato.

Isn't that funny?

I didn't laugh either. She returned to her memory, tasting it before she swallowed.

I didn't tell the babysitter. I didn't tell her I was pregnant so I figured, why tell her I'm not.

EVERY night Willa got a bedtime story. One imagined a kid who'd never been born. A Wasn't, or an Isn't. Another was about a boy whose dad had to go out. The dad said, When I come back there'll be changes. He came back with mom holding a newborn.

I read that one for the first time the night after the miscarriage. Bekah and I looked at each other. The only thing worth saying was how there was nothing to say.

The next morning was our third wedding anniversary. Willa was still asleep in her own bed. She'd slept through the night. Finally. Bekah took me in hand and guided me inside her. I tried not to think about what else was inside her.

The doctor phoned in his prescription: four black pills. They'd force Bekah to force out the embryo. She swallowed them and curled up to wait. I took Willa to the botany pond. She tiptoed up to the edge and looked down at the clouds superimposed over minnows that teemed like sperm. Between the clouds and the minnows were Willa's and my reflections, hovering on the water. Willa and I went back to the pond six months later, when a corner of its blanket of snow had melted. A dozen fish were floating upside down.

Dad. Look at the fish.

The fish are dead, I said.

Willa didn't say anything; she uttered it. It sounded like a baby garbling its first word, and a dying man rasping his last.

That was in winter. It was summer when Bekah curled up like a question mark to wait. Instead of expelling the embryo, the cramps clenched it more tightly.

The doctor was too busy to talk to her. He told his assistant to tell her to take four more pills and try again.

No, Bekah said. This is Labor Day weekend. I'm going to have my Labor Day.

She went to the beach with Willa; I went to the office to work on my book. On my living. I was writing about a guy who'd drawn comic books about the thing that got women pregnant. This had made him a criminal.

STRANGE.

That's what I said when Bekah asked me how the painter was doing. How he seemed. After he and his wife had had twins they'd moved to a bigger place on the other side of the neighborhood, but he and I had never been closer. And yet I was losing him. He'd been waxing the ends of his mustache into devilish points, checking himself in and out of the hospital, even though there was nothing wrong with him. Nothing that anyone could find. I asked him what was going on.

My childhood, he said. Now that I've got the boys, it's all coming back. I've got to deal with this so they won't have to.

I didn't know anything about his childhood; he never talked about it.

One day I bumped into him on the bike path. He was wearing the heavy-duty bike lock I'd recently sold him around one shoulder. A chain of nearly unbreakable links.

I've got your fifty dollars, he said. For the lock.

I don't care about that. How're the boys?

Great.

And you?

Not too good. He'd have to tell me about it. He'd call me. He promised to pay me for the lock.

Later that afternoon my phone rang.

Mate? Can you take me to hospital?

I drove over to his studio. He was sitting on his Afghan rug, smoking a cig. The rug had a pattern: tanks, helicopters, machine guns.

I promised myself I'd go through with it. I swore I'd do it. But I can't leave those boys. My precious, beautiful boys. Those sweet boys.

Their names were tattooed on his arms, one on each bicep.

I could leave everyone. But not them.

Leave for where?

He pointed with the end of his cig at a bag of charcoal next to the bathroom door.

Just light the bag. Seal the crack under the door. Gradual. Painless.

Silence.

It's not the wife. Things between us are good. Not perfect, but good. It's just life. You might be able to help me feel better, but then there's tonight, and tomorrow, and tomorrow night. And so. The loony bin.

Are you taking your medication?

All five. They're great.

We were surrounded by his life's work. Trading cards, each one about a nightmare he'd had. Dice, some with nouns, some with adjectives; when you rolled them you got the names he'd been called. A self-portrait titled *Idiot*. A painting of the word *idiot*. A photo of him standing next to the painting of the word *idiot*.

That's what I'd loved about him: his humor.

He handed me a black-and-white photo. Him, when he was a schoolboy. Under his necktie he'd written "1965–2008."

I picked up the charcoal.

We should go now. I'm taking this.

Yeah. Grill with it.

When we got in the car he said, I feel like a condemned man going to face his sentence.

I drove north. The streets flashed by like rows of corn.

I can't leave you and the boys, he said into his phone. So I'm going into hospital. I'm sorry. I know. Dan and Bekah said they'd help look after the boys. Bring them in tomorrow. You know how they find the place so amusing. I love you.

He clicked the phone shut.

The room is green, he said. The color of calm. Somebody put a floral band around the top of the padding. Like a little old lady wanted to brighten it up.

I stopped at a light. Cars flew by, honking.

The light's green. Dan. The light is green. Go!

I jerked the car back into gear.

I almost got you killed while I'm trying to stop you from killing yourself.

He laughed. Then he stopped.

You're sad. Don't be. I'm fine. Obviously. We're doing the right thing here.

I turned into downtown and nosed through shoppers and shiny cars.

So many happy people, he said fondly.

I pulled into the horseshoe driveway. *Emergency.* That's what this was. I had to do something, say something. But he'd already gotten out of the car. He whispered to the reception nurse, who said something to the guard. The guard blocked my way.

You can't come in. He's not allowed to speak to anyone.

A FEW days later I found one of my dictionaries on the floor. I was putting it away when I heard Bekah say, Go ask Dad.

Willa toddled into the room.

Dadda, what a ghost?

I didn't answer.

He a dead person still alive.

She hung onto the leg of a table, watching me. Waiting.

I said, A ghost lives in the spirit world.

She ran into the bedroom.

Dadda said a ghost live in the spirit world!

Spirit world. How did that come out of my mouth? I didn't believe in an afterlife. In life after death.

Or did I? I couldn't disbelieve in it. I'd tried. But it was impossible to imagine not being able to imagine anything.

The next day was Bekah's birthday. When I'd asked her what she wanted she'd said, Nothing. So we went camping. I used the painter's bag of charcoal to cook hobo stew. After we ate we huddled around the coals, watching sparks fly up.

Dadda? Where ghosts are?

Inside us. Look.

I breathed a cloud of vapor.

I mean what ghosts are.

People who're dead but don't want to be. So they haunt the living.

The firelight mutated on Willa's face. It looked like her thoughts were pulsing.

We have a good one, I said. She loves us. She loves you.

Bekah took Willa into our tent and tucked her into the mummy bag. When she came back I said that Willa was almost old enough to start remembering things, and I wanted her to remember us remembering Irene. I didn't want her to think that we'd kept her older sister a secret.

Bekah didn't say anything. She'd delivered her, I thought: She'd decide when it was time to tell Willa about her. The darkness breathed with the fire, in and out.

We looked it up in the dictionary, she said. A few days ago. Willa and I. *Ghost.* The spirit of a dead person who haunts the living.

I looked it up when we got back: also a faint or false image in a memory, mirror, or photo. The spirit of the dead, but also the living. The spirit of life itself. *Ghost* comes from *gast*, the old word for breath.

THE painter called the next day. He was out of the hospital.

You should feel good, he said. It's not every day you get to literally save someone's life.

Nine days later he hung himself on his back porch.

With a bike lock, his widow told me. So I couldn't cut him down.

No note. He'd left everything to our imagination.

His brain was dead, but the hospital was keeping his body alive until his mom and dad flew in. I could still see him if I went in today.

Today was National Pregnancy and Infant Loss

Remembrance Day. The placard in the hospital lobby said so. The painter had swollen so big his head looked shrunken. Its eyes were closed. The forehead sweated and quivered. Something inside was trying to wake up.

Hey! His widow got up and held me. It's okay; it's okay. He's not here. He's gone. This is just a body that looks like him.

But she acted like he was here. She laid a hand on his forehead and said, I'm just going to the bathroom. But Dan's here.

She nodded at a boom box.

You can put on some music.

I tried to shake my head.

Not for us, she said: for him.

She hit the play button.

This is the band that played at our wedding.

She left. I took his cold hand in mine and closed my eyes.

You never knew this, but I loved you. Loved you. From the moment I saw you at that party, when you were wearing that painting around your neck. The one that said *I'm Useless.*

I opened my eyes. My closest friend. Also the man who'd killed him. They were married now. I kissed the wet forehead.

A couple days later I put on the suit I'd worn to my wedding. Bekah and I drove to another place that called itself a home. The jar with the painter's ashes was lit by a spotlight.

The next morning Bekah took a test. Pregnant.

That night the documentarian called. The therapist had cancer. Stage four.

The next morning was my birthday. Forty years old. When we pulled up to our matchmakers' house the documentarian was raking leaves.

My son's disappeared, he said. I can't find him anywhere. Where oh where could he be?

He eyed the mound of leaves at his feet. I touched it and the leaves rustled to life. His son crawled out.

Willa said, I wanna be buried too.

We fed our kids, read them a story, and tucked them in. After the dishes the documentarian and I sat down to talk. Non-Hodgkin's lymphoma. The doctors wouldn't say what her chances were. The survival rate was somewhere between 23 and 73 percent.

Fifty-fifty, I said.

Yes. But they can't say that. They're going aggressive. They have to. The cancer's aggressive. They're—

He swallowed and stared.

They're going to come as close as they can to killing her, but without actually killing her.

After a silence he said, You only get this one life. I have everything I ever wanted. Everything.

He shook his head.

THREE days later Bekah miscarried. A heavy period. Two days later was Halloween. Willa dressed up as a witch; Bekah and I went as ourselves.

Undead kids were everywhere. One jumped out of a cauldron; another crawled out from behind a headstone. We passed a scarecrow hanging at the end of a noose. Bekah gave me a look, squeezed my hand. I steered us away from a porch full of people who'd stopped calling after Irene was born. They were holding glasses of wine and laughing. They'd been the painter's friends too. I felt even closer to him.

The next day his widow invited me over to scatter his ashes. She'd scattered half of them that morning with the twins. One had told her, I wish I could die. Then I could see Daddy again.

I climbed the stairs to their back porch. Her back porch. Two nails stuck up from the top rail. The painter had kicked at the end and sent a flower box crashing into the alley three floors down.

Raeburn, his widow called from inside. Have you ever seen human ashes?

Yes. Irene's.

Oh. Right. Sorry. It's been two years.

It had been almost four years, but I didn't say anything. She'd never written or called after the birthday, and I'd managed to kill my feelings about that. I didn't want to do anything that might bring them back to life.

The painter's best friend was in the kitchen with her. His oldest friend, from across the ocean. The other Dan. He and I shook hands; then we hugged. The three of us got on bikes and rode to a peninsula called the Point, where the Lake heaved against the limestone. The waves were the color of milky tea. The widow reached into the painter's messenger bag and pulled out a wooden box. The other Dan reached in and took out a handful. He held it for a moment, seeming to weigh something. He threw it at the Lake. Afterward he clapped his hands to his face, as though he'd just remembered that he'd forgotten something.

My fistful felt like sand and salt. I took a step and pitched it into the spray. The cloud blew back into my face. I blinked and licked my lips. They weren't tasteless. The ashes tasted like nothing, or what I imagine nothing will taste like. Like stone.

We formed a circle, bowed our heads. Nobody spoke.

When we got back to her place the widow said, I'm sorry, Dan. About Irene. About not saying anything. I couldn't bear to think about losing a child. But I should have called, or written.

She held out her arms. I hugged her so I wouldn't have to face her, and the fact that our friendship was dead.

The next day I pinned a button with a caricature of the painter on it to my jacket. Willa said his name.

I said, What's he call an avocado?

Alligator pear. He's funny.

That's the last thing she ever said about our mate. She forgot him, just like she forgot everything from those years. I didn't tell her what he'd done. I told myself I'd spare her.

Not that that was possible. She'd already heard Poppa's voice on our answering machine, choking with the news that one of his great-grandkids was dead. Six years old. Cancer. Bekah and I had stood there stricken. Willa'd popped the pacifier out of her mouth and looked at it like it was a smoldering pipe and she was a professor about to make a fine distinction.

I wanna read a book.

That's why I didn't tell her that the painter killed himself. Not because it would devastate her. Because it wouldn't.

Also because I couldn't give her a reason. There wasn't one; that's why everyone had to invent their own. Was that what I couldn't forgive? Not leaving a note? Years later I'd tell Bekah that I'd only now realized that I wasn't angry at the painter anymore.

But Bekah was angry.

He wasn't thinking of you, she said. He wasn't thinking of his friends, or his wife, or the boys. He wasn't thinking of anyone but himself, and not even that either. Obviously.

Silence.

No, she said. He was thinking of you. He truly believed everyone would be better off without him.

Another silence.

I came pretty close, she said. I can say that now. It was the sight of me more than anything. Whenever I passed a mirror.

I WAS standing in front of the bathroom mirror, holding a razor to my throat, when Bekah walked in and sat on the pot.

Still bleeding, she said. Usually my period is a few days. This has been a week. Yesterday I passed a clot. I don't think it's a new miscarriage. I think it's the last one, still. Or even the one before that. An ongoing miscarriage.

She looked down into the bowl.

Spots. Last night there was a splash.

A month later she said, Still bleeding. A month later, she said it again.

Why didn't we go to the doctor? Because she'd asked for a new one, and we were still waiting for an appointment.

Thanksgiving came. The most joyous time of the year, according to the songs on the radio and the loudspeakers lining the sidewalks. Snowflakes in the grass looked like the white hairs that now edged my temples. Every morning Willa jumped out of bed and ran to her advent calendar. She scanned the month's worth of numbered doors until she found today's, with its square of chocolate. Its gift. Her day revolved around the moment she got to eat it, just like her year revolved around the day the doors led up to. Christmas made her feel lucky to be alive.

Which she was. If Irene hadn't died on it, Willa'd be someone else, or no one at all. An Isn't.

THE cancer ward had a plastic wreath on the door. In the therapist's room, a menorah. Her turban made her look like a guru. The hollows around her eyes made the eyes inside them seem more alive, more unfazed than ever. She didn't want to talk about whether she'd live or die. She wanted to know about me and Bekah. How *were* we?

I couldn't say. The painter was dead, but his death was just getting started. The same with this miscarriage. Every day Bekah and I got up and got Willa to school, me with one death inside me, she with hers. We spent every day around each other, but we didn't really spend any time together. We saw too much of each other, and not enough. We'd never been closer. More married. And closer to divorce.

We'd argued about who was doing more around the place. Why we weren't spending more time as a family. Why the other one wouldn't just listen. At one point I'd taken Willa to the park, just to get her out of there and away from us. When I got back Bekah was gone. No note.

I'd already unloaded all this on the documentarian. He'd told me, Any family with a child under five is a family in crisis.

He would know. He and the therapist had two now: a boy and a girl. And cancer. They were the ones with the crisis. And they were the ones who got divorced. Not then, though. Not until a couple years after she'd gone into remission. When they knew for sure that she'd live. Neither of them told me why they split up. I doubt they knew.

I remembered being ten years old and hearing the phone ring.

As soon as I heard it ring I knew, my twin told me. I just knew. It was Mom. She wasn't coming back, and she was going to take us with her: to Oregon, Alaska, Texas. Wherever the preacher decided to go next.

He'd overheard our dad lift the receiver from its cradle. Silence, then the sound of a grown man choking. Also a baby crying. My twin's never forgotten the sound. Neither have I, even though I've never heard it, only heard my twin talk about it. After our dad hung up he rushed upstairs and gathered us into his arms, to hold what he'd had, but hadn't realized.

The countdown neared zero. The light grew thin. Instead of remembering Irene's birthday, I remembered remembering it. Like the time I'd been digging through our linen drawer and come across the diaper Bekah had had to wear. The brown bloodstains had looked like continents on a map. I'd reburied it in the drawer. I went back and unpacked the drawer but the diaper was gone. The one thing that could show me the way back to that day we came home from the hospital. Before we had to start seeing people again.

People. Bekah's aunts' annual Christmas party was that night. I didn't want to go. Neither did Bekah, but she went. She came back early. She was still bleeding. It had been four years since Irene had kicked at that party, and Bekah had woken up the next morning with a headache. She woke up the next morning with a headache.

I'm coming down with something.

She spent the shortest day of the year making soup. She ladled it into bowls and excused herself. I followed her into our bedroom and tried to get her to sit up and take some aspirin. She murmured, already asleep. I felt like I was the one who was asleep. Like I was dreaming, and knew that I was dreaming, but couldn't believe it enough to wake up.

I read Willa her goodnight story. In the morning I asked Bekah how she felt.

Depressed.

She walked out of the room. Her headache got worse.

Eat, I said.

Quit hectoring me.

That did it. For weeks we'd felt like ghosts; now we'd make a scene. A drama our drama didn't really have. A substance. A reason for it. As we fought I couldn't shake the sense that we were making sure that Irene wouldn't die alone. We'd sacrifice the marriage that had made her, and we'd do it by re-creating the ones that had made us.

Bekah finally stopped bleeding on Christmas Eve. That's the day her mom arrived, carrying a dollhouse with a wooden family inside it. She left on Irene's birthday. She didn't mention her. Neither did Bekah. Neither did I. Our fourth Christmas since Irene's birthday and our fourth pregnancy, or bout of pregnancies. I was glad the embryo was dead. If there'd been two I was glad both were dead.

That night the three of us went for a walk along the Lake. The light from the streetlamps tinged the snow blue. By the time we got to the Point we were numb. We hurried to a Japanese restaurant. After hot noodle soup we let Willa have three scoops of green tea ice cream. She ate them happily, like a girl at her birthday party.

Wait, I said. Is there caffeine in green tea ice cream?

There was. A lot. Willa jumped into her parka and twirled her arms in circles. The mittens attached to her cuffs spun around like airplane propellers.

I'm winding up! she said. Winding up!

She ran out the door.

Winding up! Winding up!

Bekah and I had to chase her all the way back to our place. We had to laugh. She'd made us.

Five

WE MADE OUR FIFTH ONE THREE WEEKS LATER, after another walk along the Lake. The waves were gray, the sky white. Willa was asleep in her stroller. We sat on a bench and stared at the water the way we stare at the ceiling when we're in bed, summoning thoughts.

Why did I bring up our firstborn? Because I didn't want to, not really. Talking about her felt like talking about someone behind her back. Betraying her, or betraying myself. I couldn't tell the difference anymore.

Irene. The name sounded strange out loud. Maybe Bekah would say it too, make it sound like more than the voice in my head.

I said that when I'd held Irene, I had no idea how much we'd lost. Now I did. My understanding had grown, just like Willa had grown, just like Irene would've grown if she'd lived. Instead of ending Irene's death, Willa's life was making it seem real. Palpable.

I paused. The words sounded too big and too small. Too much like words.

Bekah was quiet. When her baby died, a part of her died. A real part, not part of her psyche. If Irene was still alive in me, it's because she'd never been actually alive in me. She'd been an idea. Now she'd always be one.

That night we made love. The little death, people used to call it. It had the same rhythm as birth: pushing, thrusting, climax. Instead of a baby crying, we sounded like we were dying.

Three days later one of Bekah's uncles killed himself. At our wedding he'd pressed an envelope into my hand and squeezed it. I'd forgotten his face, but not what he looked like. Not that squeeze. Now I'd never forget them, or him. Suicide gives you a long life.

His funeral was held in the town where Bekah was born. When she got back from it she took a test: pregnant. I tried to be excited. Two weeks later, there was blood in her underwear. I tried to be disappointed.

Later that day my cell phone rang.

Guess what?

I was out of guesses.

I'm pregnant.

Positive. She'd taken another test.

Hon. You just had your period this morning.

It's not a period. It's an implantation. The embryo attached to the uterus. Attaching can cause bleeding. Spotting, which is all I've had. The blood's actually a good sign.

Silence.

You're probably not ready to let yourself get excited yet.

No, I was ready to feel something. Anything. I wasn't worried that the embryo was dead; I was worried that I was dead.

We agreed not to tell Willa, not yet. Bekah went to her first ultrasound by herself; I took Willa to a museum nearby. It has fetuses in jars. I steered away from those. We went downstairs to the hatchery, where we watched a chick peck its way out of its egg. It fell over and lay still.

It's just sleeping, the girl next to Willa said.

Yeah, the girl's dad said. Sleeping.

He winked at me.

Next, The Miracle of Life. Touch any chromosome to begin. An egg-shaped theater showing a movie about a fish whose roe streamed out like jam. A biologist basted it with milt. The hallway out of the theater led us to an exhibit about the moon shot. Ominous music, grave narration. The lander with only seconds of fuel remaining. A pause, then the announcement: The Eagle has landed.

Right then my cell phone rang.

Alive and well. All systems go.

Bekah's voice was broken, like it was transmitted from space. Which it was.

Due on October 14th.

Halfway between her birthday and mine. Someone half her, half me. A coincidence. Why were coincidences the only thing making me feel like I'd be a dad again?

The photo of the ultrasound looked like a cutaway view of a brain. Bekah stuck it to our refrigerator. On the first day of spring Willa pointed and said, What's that.

Bekah looked at me. I held up my empty hands.

My tummy, Bekah said.

What's that inside your tummy.

A baby.

Willa patted the mound under Bekah's belly button.

Where's the baby?

Then she clapped her hands to her cheeks.

Will *I* be the baby?

No. You'll be the big sister. Being a big sister is fun. I'm a big sister.

Willa listed the things she'd teach the baby to do: talk, read, eat, cook. Play ghost.

She started to cry: *I* won't be the baby.

Bekah scooped her up, molded her to her chest.

You'll always be my baby. You'll always be my first.

That made me feel like a dad. Like Irene's dad.

In June one of Bekah's sisters gave birth. A girl. Two weeks later another sister gave birth. Another girl. Both born naturally, with no inducements, no drugs, no interventions, both on their due date, or next to it. Two things could create a third: three girls born to three sisters, in one year. And a dad starting to feel like he'd be a dad again. I told my boss that Bekah and I were expecting. A girl. He was surprised I'd said anything.

Bekah and I drove up to the North Side to buy a double stroller.

Getting cocky, I said.

A pandemic was imminent, or declared imminent. Flu, one that could do what the last big one did and kill more people than every war in history combined. I knew this, but I didn't actually believe it. I turned off the radio and took Willa downtown, where the crowds were, or would've been if it hadn't been for what people were saying on the radio. Willa was wearing her tutu and her tiara and singing Jingle Bells. Rudolph the Red-Nosed Reindeer. People couldn't help but smile. She was infectious.

An old man in a guayabera shirt took the cigar out of his mouth and said, Happy Farther's Day.

Farther's Day. Father's Day was two days away, but he was right. It had taken me half my life to get to this point. No, my whole life. Today was my day, the one the rest'll be based on. Tufts floated down from the cottonwood trees.

There was no line to get into the museum. Footsteps echoed off the marble. The handful of tourists under the Tyrannosaur were wearing the same masks as the people who'd delivered Willa and Irene. I took Willa into the exhibit that begins with the water that covers everything. A volcano erupts; that, or a meteor strikes. Something makes a bacterium invade a cell. The bacterium rewrites the cell's instructions, reauthorizing it. It splits into two, four, eight, until it's something new, then newer, until the water's moving with a trillion things. One's a fish who can't survive, so she stumps her way onto land. This failure makes her human. It leads to turtles that lay their eggs in the sand. Reptiles become dinosaurs, dinosaurs birds. Rats mastodons, apes men. These eras begin and end with red zones: *Mass Extinction*. Climate changes: They're part of a pattern. The bigger you are, the more likely it is you'll die out. Only the small survive, and only what's too small to see with the naked eye survives unchanged. The meek keep reinheriting the earth.

We come to the Ice Age that's left behind the Lake, and a skeleton. An ape who isn't an ape, not anymore. Someone's buried her. Proof that whoever's buried her isn't a hominid. He's human.

He's buried her in a pothole, in the fetal position.

THE solstice was Father's Day. The longest day of the year. Willa and I spent it in bed with a fever of 103 degrees. I stroked her skull and stared at the moon out our window. Clouds appeared and disappeared, transforming without really changing. After seven nights, two trips to the doctor, and one round of antibiotics, Willa still had the flu. So did I. So did Bekah. I had to wait for her to stop coughing before I could go back to reading Willa her bedtime story.

The painter's birthday passed. So did our country's. We didn't leave the apartment. It sounded like a war zone out there. One night I found Bekah bent over a puddle: She'd coughed so hard that she peed herself. Later I woke up to another splash. I found her doubled over, like she'd been shot.

Don't go to work tomorrow, I said. I know the show has to go on. But that's my point: It'll go on without you.

We need the money.

No we don't.

Not true, but I needed to be able to tell myself that we'd done all we could. So the reason would be swine flu, not her working too hard.

She slept naked on top of our sheets. I woke up staring at her heart-shaped rear. Still as soft and white as when she'd been a baby. Something was sticking out of the crack between her cheeks. Something small, round, milky. A pearl?

She woke up and went to the bathroom. When she came back she didn't say anything. Neither did I. She tucked panty liners into her purse and went to work. The soldier again.

That afternoon she nearly blacked out at the post office.

She called the new doctor. Please, she said: When I fell down coughing today I had some sharp pains in my womb. No, not my chest. My womb. They were separate from the coughing. They were sharp, in my uterus. I've had some discharge. I'm afraid my mucus plug might've come out.

The receptionist was sorry; the hospital wasn't admitting anyone who had the flu.

Bekah fell in and out of sleep. When I put my hand on her mound her eyes opened.

Still moving, she said. Just not now.

July passed; so did the flu. Then it came back. Then it

went away again. The fetus kept moving. August. September. On October 1st Bekah woke up and said, My hands are still asleep.

She kneaded them with each other.

They're numb. Like before.

I put my hand on her mound.

Still moving, she said. But not as much.

She called the new doctor. The new doctor had quit; we'd have to wait until the hospital assigned a new one. She called her general physician: The soonest she could get an appointment was in more than a month. We thought about the emergency room. Would hands going to sleep in the night count as an emergency?

The last time they tested my thyroid they lowered my dosage, she said. I'm going back to my old dose.

She ate a pill, then snapped another in half. She snapped a half in half and ate one of the crumbs. The next morning the numbness wasn't as present.

The new doctor didn't want to hear about Bekah's hands. She didn't have time to hear everything that had brought us to this point. She wanted to induce labor as soon as possible. The soonest she could do it was at the end of week thirty-seven, ten days from now.

Okay, Bekah said. But I thought that it wasn't recommended to induce labor in a woman who's had a cesarean before. That's what my last doctor said, and the doctor before that. My doula, too.

Then you can have a cesarean. We don't want another stillbirth on our hands.

The next day was Bekah's birthday. Forty. We took a walk in the woods. Willa collected leaves Bekah put in her pockets. My pockets; she was wearing my goose down vest again. She looked bigger than ever in it, and smaller than ever. More precious than ever.

The life in her didn't feel like it was hers, she said. Not to anyone but her. Nothing was natural; everything was political. Insurance policies, hospital policies, liability policies. And this new doctor. Instead of waiting for Bekah's water to break, they'd break it manually. They'd use drugs to make her uterus contract. Forced contractions hurt more, so they'd give her painkillers. The painkillers would make her numb, so they'd use more drugs to induce more forceful contractions.

This wasn't a special plan; this was the standard birth plan, and the woman insisting on it was about to become the first person on earth to touch our daughter.

Bekah called our doula. The doula said that there was nothing that said Bekah had to listen to her doctor. She could just stop going to the weekly ultrasounds and non-stress tests. Just wait until she was in labor, then show up.

That was a thought. The question was, was it one we could live with?

Bekah told the doctor that she wanted to give birth naturally. The doctor said that that all depended; she'd have to have a look at the next ultrasound.

If I see anything less than absolutely perfect, I'm sending you to Labor and Delivery.

The ultrasound showed that the fetus was alive and well. All systems go. But when Bekah got back to our apartment there was already a message on our answering machine: Be at Labor and Delivery tomorrow morning.

When Bekah called to ask why the secretary said, Failure to thrive.

She sounded like she was reading it off a sheet.

Can you tell me why? Bekah said.

The secretary didn't have that information.

Is the doctor planning to induce me?

Yes.

Everything I've read, and everyone I've talked to, including other doctors in your own practice, has said that it's not recommended to chemically induce labor in a woman who's had a c-section.

We do. It's not a big deal. What time would you like to be induced.

I wouldn't. I don't want another c-section either. But

I'd rather do that than do something that might be more dangerous. So let's make an appointment for a c-section. As soon as possible.

That turned out to be the day after tomorrow: our original due date, halfway between Bekah's birthday and mine.

Bekah was dispirited. She wanted another one after this, but I didn't. I was ready to stop having kids and start raising them, and being able to afford them. She'd probably lost her last chance at giving birth. At the travail. At war with the universe; not to beat it, but to become one with it. The twenty-eight hours it had taken her to deliver Irene had almost killed her, but it had also saved her. It had delivered her, too.

It's not about me, she said. One more unnatural childbirth isn't a tragedy. But millions?

We were listening to Congress argue about health insurance. Congress: the perfect name for those fuckers. If they'd passed the law half of them were arguing against now five years earlier, Bekah could've seen a doctor before she was pregnant with Irene, not after. Before it was already too late.

On Easter Sunday I'd picked up the *Times*. It said that women who had Bekah's thyroid condition had more babies who died. Lots more. Women should get their thyroid checked before they get pregnant, or as soon as they find out they're pregnant, not after.

I don't remember Bekah's reaction to this news. Did we really want a reason for Irene's death? If we'd had her, we wouldn't have Willa.

Also because Irene didn't die on Christmas, or on Christmas Eve. She died on the day after Christmas. The autopsy said so.

"Forty-eight to seventy-two hours dead," it read. "Died on the 26th or earlier."

Or earlier. It had to be earlier. That kicking at the party: Those were her death throes. If they weren't, she was still alive when I drove us to my dad's house. When Bekah and I woke up in my old bedroom. Instead of going for that walk to the kiln, we could've gone to the emergency room. There'd been one five minutes away. Mercy. I knew the way by heart.

I couldn't live with that, so I didn't. When the doctor read the numbers to me over the phone I wrote them down in my desk calendar, not to remember them, but to put them out of my mind. Literally. Until four and a half years later, when I reopened my daily planner.

"48–72 hours dead." In ink, in my own hand.

I must've forgot in order to protect Bekah. Must've. My voice cracked as I told her the truth.

You never talked to the doctor, she said. I did. I was the one who called you with the results. That was me you talked to.

Then I remembered. Not her saying the words; me hearing them. The shock of what they implied, the shock that also killed that implication. I remembered my memory dying at the moment it was born.

Bekah's didn't die. That's why she nearly killed herself, and I didn't.

WHY didn't we go to the emergency room? Maybe if we'd had insurance. But state aid wasn't any good out of state; insurance companies had made sure of that. Drug companies too. Doctors. Lawyers. Investors. The stock market. Our country. Our culture killed her. Christmas too: the party on the eve of Christmas Eve, then on the Eve. Then again first thing in the morning under the tree. Then the dinner I'll never remember. After all those parties you wake up and realize that it hadn't been a dream; that you'd spent yesterday expecting the baby to kick at any moment. But if you say anything about it, you ruin Christmas. So you make small talk. That killed her. That silence. Hers and mine, the next morning at breakfast. We killed her.

Irene saved her mom's life twice. First by the court in the park, then again in the endocrinologist's office, with that little silver hammer. She died of the disorder she'd made us aware of. She died inside Bekah, and instead of Bekah. In her place.

And this was how we'd repaid her.

It was easier to believe that than the truth, which is that she died for all these reasons and more. Of the thyroid, the urinary tract infections, the gestational diabetes, the heart-shaped uterus. White matter, dark matter. Congress. Of everything in the world, and nothing in particular. Of life, the thing that kills everyone, and for one reason: because once upon a time, two people met and made love.

That was the same as no reason at all. It was easier to believe that I was responsible. Isn't that what dads are supposed to be?

THE day of the cesarean was overcast. Wet leaves stuck to the sidewalk. We buckled Willa into her stroller.

Our last walk as a trio, I said. And a quartet.

Bekah's mom had driven more than a thousand miles overnight to be with us. We walked Willa to her nursery school and told her that we loved her. She'd heard it all before. She ran off to play.

Stepping into the hospital felt like stepping onto an ocean liner. Generators thrumming somewhere. Doctors striding by like captains; orderlies pushing mops. Crews of nurses at their station. Each room was a cabin, with a sink, a window, and a patient waiting patiently. For what?

Bicornuate uterus. Heterozygous prothrombin mutation. Calcified uterine mass.

A resident was reading Bekah's history.

Heart murmur.

He took off his stethoscope.

Just picked up on that one.

Miscarriage December '08. C-section May '06. Stillbirth December '04. Miscarriage December '03.

The plotline. I remembered Bekah saying, This isn't me. I'm not myself.

A woman in a white coat walked in and looked me in the eye.

Your doctor couldn't be here today. I'm the doctor.

Bekah's eyes opened wide, met mine.

The doctor offered me her hand: dark brown with a cool, pink palm. I wanted to take it in both of mine and squeeze it. She followed the orderlies wheeling Bekah out of the room. I was alone with Bekah's mom.

That was a little hard for me, she said.

They'd wheeled her baby boy away like that. The next time she saw him he was dead.

I, of all people, should've had something to say to this. I'd seen Irene wheeled away like that. But I didn't say a word, just like everyone I'd ever been mad at. Like an idiot.

An orderly came back with my paper suit. Bekah's mom would have to wait in the waiting room; parents were allowed in the theater, but not parents of parents.

This your first?

Third, I said. Second living.

She led me into the theater. Bekah's head stuck out from under the blue screen. I sat next to it.

Her hand, a masked man said. We arranged her hand for you.

I took it. It felt refrigerated.

Hi.

Hi.

What'd you and Mom talk about?

Your brother.

Yeah. We finally had a talk about all that last night.

A hose twitched. Pink froth sprayed into the canister behind Bekah's head: one hundred milliliters. Two hundred. Three hundred.

The masked men were talking about Iowa City. One of them had been offered a job there; he thought he'd like living there. The other one said he wouldn't. No way.

Something yowled. Bekah's pupils eclipsed their irises.

A voice said, She's not even out yet.

Another yowl.

Look, Dad.

A violet monster at the end of a rope. A nurse snipped the rope and the monster turned red. Into an imp. The nurse laid it under a heat lamp.

What's her Apgar?

She's a ten.

Can't be. We never give tens around here.

She bit me!

They gave her a ten.

When I leaned over my girl she pulled my mask from my face and looked at me without seeing me, like I was a mirror that didn't have a reflection in it. I slid my hands under her and her arms shot up, panicked. It had been a year since I'd held the painter's hand in this hospital; my newborn wouldn't remember what I was saying either. I was talking to myself.

You're the luckiest girl in the world, I said. I stroked her skull.

The doctor had her arm up to its elbow inside Bekah. Bekah said, I have a bicornuate uterus.

I know. I'm looking at it. Reach your hand up there, she said to the man next to her: You can feel the hole leading to the other side.

Bekah's mom was in the waiting room with Willa.

Willa's eyes were green and brown at once. Olive, or hazel. We'd thought about Olive, but we'd named our newborn Hazel.

I told Willa what I'd been afraid to tell her:

You have a sister.

Willa nodded. Barely, as though she'd known all along.

ELEVEN days later was my birthday. Forty-one. I woke up to the whorl of hair on the back of Hazel's head. She was attached to Bekah's breast. Willa climbed into bed and inserted herself between us. Irene's urn was above us. I didn't have everything I ever wanted, but I had everything I wanted to want. More than I'd ever wanted. I was the luckiest guy in the world.

One of Bekah's aunts came for dinner. After we put the girls to bed the aunt told us about Bekah's great-grandma, Mahmoo. Mahmoo's first baby got stuck on its way out. For a day and a half the top of its head sat between her legs. The doctor took her husband aside.

You have to choose between her and the baby.

Her.

The doctor drilled a hole into the baby's skull. He sucked out its brains with a syringe. That's how Mahmoo was delivered.

We stared at the remains of my birthday dinner.

The baby was still alive, Bekah said. When they drilled into it.

Yes. Not for long, one would hope.

When we got undressed that night Bekah said, If they hadn't done that I wouldn't exist.

Another thing I'd never want, and couldn't imagine life without.

THE one thing I wanted now was time. There was so much less of it. After Willa was born we'd taken naps. Long strolls along the Lake. We'd bonded with her, and with each other. The day after Hazel's birthday I had to teach a three-hour class on I don't remember what. Probably memory; that's what all memoirs were about. Bekah and I got up while it was still dark out to put away dishes, make breakfast, and pack lunches. We got Willa up and got her to eat and go to the bathroom. To brush her teeth, put on underwear and pants, a shirt and sweater. Snow pants, boots, coat, hat. Mittens. Scarf. Don't forget your backpack. All while fighting her almost every step of the way, all before eight in the morning, with Hazel grieving loudly. Two kids were making us do twice as much, making us faster than ever.

Both of us had them, but Bekah had them more. One night I came back to the apartment too late to help with dinner. I'd stopped off at a friend's for a beer. I'd called, and when Bekah didn't answer, I'd had another. And another. I walked into the kitchen happy.

Bekah had a wooden spoon in one fist.

You're turning into my dad.

And you're turning into your mom.

She went into the half room and slammed the door. I heard her make up a bed and type.

It wasn't her dad I was worried about turning into. It was mine. The one who'd lost custody of his kids. Six months later I'd read what she'd typed that night. I'd scroll through her emails, looking for a tax form, and see the subject line: *Fight*.

It said she was sick of me. That she was going to leave me and take the girls with her. Not now, but soon. As soon as she could afford it.

I'd reread the words, aware I'd never believe them, knowing I'd have to.

THE shortest day of the year. The snowflakes floated like the cottonwood tufts at midsummer. Bekah had taken Willa and Hazel down South to see their cousins, leaving me alone so I could write. I wasn't writing about comics anymore. Now I was writing about the stillbirth. About Irene. Again. Actually I'd been writing about her all this time in secret, in my notebooks. Now the secret was out. I was turning it into a book.

Starting now. But first I had to clean our room. I stripped our bed and fitted it with fresh sheets, polished the photo of our joint self. The glass squeaked. I cleaned everything but the urn. It had grown a gray fleece. Dust and lint. I picked it up and sneezed. I walked it to the kitchen table and set it down and sponged it. Gently, the way I'd sponged Bekah after Irene was born. It shone like an eye that's blinked. When I pulled the cork out the urn tilted and the ash inside hissed.

I lowered my nose and sniffed. Nothing. Then something faint, faintly sulfurous. Burned eggshell. I stuck the cork into the eye and put the urn back on its shelf. Why did I feel closer to Irene now than I did when I'd poured her into it? Closer than I did when she wasn't even dead yet?

I sat on the edge of the bed. This was where we made her. After she was born, it's where we retreated. Where we repaired. She was already where she belonged. At home.

According to a writer from Bekah's old neighborhood, death's like the black backing behind a mirror: It lets us reflect on what would otherwise be see-through. After

Irene died we'd had to get dressed and go to work. To act like she'd never been born. The act had nearly killed us, until the day someone asked, How're you? and we realized that we *were* okay. It wasn't an act anymore. The lie had come true.

This urn was all I had left of her. This totem. I wanted her sisters to pour my ashes into it too. To make her resting place mine.

I wiped up the ring the urn had left on the kitchen table. In the middle was the bowl Bekah had given me, holding a dozen oranges. A still life. I went into the living room and turned on the lights around our tree. Tonight Bekah and the girls were due at the airport. We'd tuck in the girls, then slide into bed together. I could already feel her legs sliding against mine. Feel the thing that started everything.

The next morning I took Willa to the aquarium. The sign outside said, *It's a Boy.* Born Saturday, five foot six, 152 pounds. My size. A sheet of paper taped to the ticket window said that the whales were closed to the public. I asked an usher why.

Family time.

She had her hands behind her back, determined to control the crowd, but also something inside herself.

Tomorrow's newspaper would confirm my hunch: The calf had died. For no apparent reason.

I took Willa's hand. Let's go see the sharks instead.

Dad. Why can't we see the baby?

Because I want your childhood to live a little longer. Because I'm afraid to tell you that you have an older sister who'll always be younger than you. An elder.

I'll tell you why, I said.

I squatted and looked her in the eye.

The baby died.

But they'll be some new babies later.

I hope so.

I stood and pushed the down button on the elevator. When the doors dinged open Willa said, All babies die.

Firmly, like it was a rule she had to remember.

CHRISTMAS morning the four of us opened presents. It wasn't our first Christmas at home, but it was our first with no relatives at all.

Our first alone, we said. Our first as a family.

For dinner we did something we'd never done on Christmas: We went out to eat. To a restaurant. Bekah knew a place in Chinatown. I studied the crowd.

It had to happen, I said. We've turned into Jews.

I thought Bekah would smile, but she didn't. Something stopped her. She ordered the salt and pepper crab; Willa got shrimp toast. I had clams. We shared it all while Hazel slept in her safety seat.

When we went to bed Bekah said she felt a little off. In the morning she was pale.

I'm coming down with something.

She took two aspirin. That night we put on a dinner party: pizza for a couple other couples and our kids. The minute everyone left Bekah fell asleep. When she woke up in the night she realized she'd shit herself. In the morning it was her underwear drying on the radiator, not Willa's.

She and Hazel slept face to face all day, like reflections. Their lips were gray and cracked. Hazel's chin trembled when she tried to nurse. I took Willa to the cartoonist's birthday party; the biology teacher was throwing it a day early. When she opened the door for us I saw that I wasn't the only one remembering the last time I'd shown up without Bekah.

It's just shellfish, I said.

I wanted to believe this, but the three of us had shared everything.

I don't remember the party or the bedtime story I fell asleep reading. I woke up in the middle of the night.

Something gushing. Our toilet. I heard Bekah gasp and flush. She brushed her teeth and creaked down the hall.

Irene's birthday wasn't really a day. It grew gray, not light. I had to keep the bulbs burning so I could read the instructions to Willa's new toys. In the bedroom Bekah's and Hazel's breath rose and fell like waves hissing over sands. In the middle of the afternoon it was night again.

The phone rang. My mom. She'd be here in two days. She gave me her flight times. Bekah's mom called. She didn't mention Irene either.

Neither did I. I wore Willa in a backpack so I could talk to her over my shoulder while I washed dishes and sponged away what had freckled the bowl of our toilet. I was picking up the litter of half-naked dolls I'd been stepping over all day when one's eyelashes fluttered open. I buried the thing at the bottom of a basket. I emptied the bucket on Bekah's side of the bed and gave Willa her dinner. I brushed her hair and teeth and got her into her pajamas and read her her bedtime story. Back to the sink. Time to wash more flecks from more dishes.

It was like she'd never been born.

The first time I asked Bekah when she wanted to tell Willa about Irene, she said, I haven't really thought about it that much. I didn't realize what my mom went through until I had Willa, and Willa's not going to realize what we went through until she's had her own.

But a few days after Hazel's first birthday, an acquaintance of Bekah's told her that today was her son's birthday. This woman didn't have a son. She'd wondered when she and her husband should tell their daughter that she didn't have a brother. They didn't want to tell her when she was older; she'd think that they'd been keeping him a secret. But they didn't want to tell her now, when she was too young to understand what the secret was. Now was too soon, and soon it'd be too late.

Bekah said, Do you think we should tell Willa now?

The two of us were nested together in bed, in the dark.

I did. I said that the only thing that could make it worse would be pretending it never happened. It was better than nothing. It had given us something. A familiar. A ghost.

I wouldn't do that, Bekah said. She's not old enough to understand what a ghost is. She knows that it's a spirit of the dead that haunts the living, but she doesn't know what death is.

I wasn't so sure. One time I'd been telling Willa about something that had happened before she was born, and she'd cut me off by saying, When I was dead.

Another time the four of us had been at the Point,

watching the sun set. Pink clouds, purple skyscrapers. The Lake breeze. Willa said, Mom, when did I die?

What? You didn't.

Why?

Bekah looked at the skyline.

Good question.

Bekah said she wanted to tell Willa after Hazel was asleep, so we could give her our full attention in the aftermath. Also on a Friday night, so she'd have the weekend to take it all in before she had to go back to school. But next Friday we were too busy; we were always too busy. Before the next Friday could come and go Willa said, Mom? Was I your first baby?

Bekah stopped what she was doing. Picking up a toy, probably.

No. I had a baby before you. Her name was Irene. But she was born dead.

Why?

Nobody knows.

Something came over her, Bekah told me: just for a second. It was the opposite of a faraway look. A nearaway look, if there is such a thing. Like she was looking in and at nothing at the same time. And then just as sudden she was back. Her old self again, off and running with her patter: But I was the first baby to come home with you. I was the first to have nah-nah with you. I was the first to go to school. And so on.

Bekah was standing naked in front of the bathroom mirror. I was floating in the tub.

I'm sorry I told her without you there. But the question was right there in front of me, with Willa watching.

You did the right thing. You said what I would've.

So had Willa, who hadn't said anything about Irene. She didn't always obey us, but she always imitated us.

THE next day I took Willa to the library. The first book we saw on the shelves was *Brave Irene.*

Yeah!

Willa grabbed it and held it in front of her. The title was upside down in her eyeglasses.

I said, Did Mom talk to you about her?

Yes.

She told you what happened.

Willa nodded.

What happened?

She died.

Willa sagged after she'd said it, like a puppet whose

strings had gone slack. Then she straightened up and walked down the aisle, running her hand along the spines, parroting titles.

It was the saddest thing in the whole world, I said.

Willa stopped and turned.

Why?

Good question. I couldn't imagine having Irene instead of Willa and Hazel. Not having the two luckiest girls in the world.

Because, I said. We loved her, just like we love you. When she died we felt the same way we'd feel if . . .

I trailed off. Willa went back to the spines.

I DON'T know when Bekah told Hazel about Irene. Sometime before a day when Hazel was four, when we took her and Willa to a temple on the North Shore. Not for the religion; for the architecture. On the drive there we passed the hospital where Irene and Willa were born.

That's where I threw pots.

Bekah nodded at the art center on the other side of the road. She turned around in her seat to look back at the girls.

Including the special one. The one with your sister's ashes in it.

Hazel said, Can I see?

After dinner Hazel asked again. Bekah handed her the urn.

You put the cork in it?

Dad did. To keep your sister's ashes in.

How did she die?

Nobody knows.

But when did she die?

Before you were born. Before both of you were born.

Was she my sister?

Yes.

Where is she?

In there.

You burned her all up?

Only her body. Only after she died.

Why?

Some people want to be buried in the ground when they die. Other people want to be burned to ash.

She wanted to be *burned*?

No, but we did. We wanted to keep her ashes. And this is where we keep them. This is where they'll always be. Careful, honey.

Hazel had her cheek pressed to the urn. She was fluttering her eyelashes.

It's sad.

Talk about something else! Willa said. Change the subject!

Willa was holding her head between her hands. Hazel got down from her chair, still holding the urn.

Honey, Bekah said. Give me that.

No.

Bekah reached for the urn. Hazel spun away.

What should have happened next didn't. Bekah got the urn and put it back in its place.

Its resting place. That's why I'm telling this story. The morning after Bekah had asked me in bed if I thought we should tell Willa about Irene, I'd gotten up and noticed that Irene's ashes were gone. Their shelf too. Nothing was above her side of the bed.

Jesus. If our apartment was on fire, those ashes would be the first possession I'd save. I wanted to shout, Bekah! but she'd already left for work. I was alone. More alone than I'd have been if the urn was where it was supposed to be. I found it in the hallway bookcase, tucked between hardcovers. I never asked Bekah why she'd moved it. There couldn't be a reason. This wasn't a matter of reason.

Which is why I was struck dumb that night after we went to the temple, when Hazel asked if she could see the pot with her sister in it. Bekah had turned to me and said, Where's the urn with Irene's ashes?

She'd forgotten. I couldn't believe it. I couldn't speak. Only point at the bookshelf.

But none of those endings had happened yet on Irene's fourth birthday. Fifth birthday. The one where it felt like she'd never been born. The only thing that happened that day, other than cleaning, was nothing. I couldn't cry. That's what was sad.

I knew this would happen. Even on the night Irene was born I knew I'd live again. Be normal. It was unthinkable, and inevitable. That's why I'd grieved: for her death, but also for the death of her death. Because even then I knew that I wouldn't be able to now. Bekah knew it too. Three weeks after Irene was born she said, I'm afraid of going back to my former self.

We had no right to cry anyway. Irene hadn't had a life. We had nothing to mourn.

And today was her birthday. How could I honor the hand she'd had in me? She was already in her resting place. I didn't have another ritual to fill. The only thing I could do wasn't for her. Not on her behalf, not in her memory. In her name only. I opened our laptop and donated money in her name to an art center, where kids could be safe from other kids. I gave bees to a family that could sell their honey.

Chicks to a kid who'd eat their eggs, or them. I gave lives to strangers.

My mom came. After Bekah and the girls were asleep she was telling me about the importance of being in The Now. The Present.

The future, I said. That's what having kids has made me think about. Sacrificing now so the girls'll benefit later.

Sacrifice. That's an awful word.

It is. That's why it's the root of *sacred.*

No. I don't believe that. That's not true.

Look it up. Abraham's willingness to sacrifice his son. God's willingness to sacrifice his son. That's why he's the sacrifice to end all sacrifices. Why his death's the death of death. His birth too. That's the real meaning of Christmas. That's what this is all about. The death of a child is supposed to give us life after death.

I was waving my arms.

We send our kids to the other side of the world to fight a war that isn't even necessary, I said. That's completely invented. When those kids come back in a box we don't say, He lost his life, or, His life was taken from him. We say he *gave* his life. We use the word *sacrifice.* Always. War is sacred too. Unfortunately.

My mom was speechless. I could tell I'd hurt her. On accident, or on purpose?

Both. She'd delivered me into this. Who else could I blame?

ON the last day of the year Bekah was well enough to walk around the apartment. She stood at the kitchen window watching the light drain out of the day.

I heard this story on the radio, she said. It was about a photographer who volunteered to photograph this couple with their dead baby.

I stopped washing the plate in my hands.

I was so disoriented when you handed her to me, she said. Hearing about that photograph and how grateful those parents were; it made me think it'd be good to have something to remember her by. But then I remember her tone. I think about a photograph of me looking at her, saying hello and goodbye at the same time, and I think, No.

She was still staring out the window. Thin lines joined the folds around her eyes to her ears, nose, and mouth.

You know how when you read a book? You can't see what's happening. But you see it anyway. You complete the picture. From memory. And my memories from that time; they're so rich and compassionate. A photograph might take away from that. It takes away what you provide. And I prefer to provide it.

She turned to me and said, It cemented us.

It did. She never did leave me and take the girls with her, even after she could afford it. We're still together. We survived losing a child, and we survived having them.

The night I found the letter that said she was going to leave me, I closed Bekah's laptop and stared at the floor. After a while I walked into the bedroom and sat on the edge of our bed. It was empty; Bekah and the girls were at grandma's for the night.

We weren't married; we were stuck together. That's what *cemented* meant.

I did something I'd never done before. I got down on my knees. I closed my eyes and pressed my palms against each other. I made my hands twins.

Please, I said. Please.

I didn't say it out loud. I said it to myself, like someone other than me could read my mind. An empty gesture. I didn't believe in God. I didn't believe in anything. Who was I talking to? No one.

That's you. Irene. The one who doesn't exist. The no one. The one who gave *me* life.

Like all parents, I worship my kids.

THANKS

To Sven Birkerts, Tom Bissell, Susan Cheever, Nick Flynn, Debra Gwartney, Phillip Lopate, Bob Shacochis, and Mark Slouka, who read this when it was an embryo; to Jim Rutman and Bob Weil, who delivered it; and to David Remnick and Deborah Treisman, who adopted it. To Matt Weiland, who helped me raise it. Also to Katherine Karvunis, the MacDowell Colony, the Vermont Studio Center, the Howard Foundation at Brown University, and the National Endowment for the Arts, who gave me time and room to labor. To Vu Tran and Chris Ware, who listened. To Willa and Hazel, who made me listen. But most of all to Rebekah, who carried me.